The Clam Lover's Cookbook

THIRD EDITION

by

William G. Flagg

N NORTH RIVER PRESS, INC.

Manufactured in the United States of America.

Library of Congress Cataloging in Publication Data

Flagg, William G,. 1934–
    The clam lover's cookbook.

    1. Cookery (Clams) I. Title.
TX753.F52 1983   641.6'94   83-2445
ISBN 0-88427-054-8

CREDITS

Many thanks are due to Penny Carter, an artist at the Rhode Island School of Design, for the sketches of "Sam" the Clam. Also, to Marilyn Holmes, for her help in verifying both technical data and text. Last, but by no means least, the continued faith of my Mom (and don't we all need that), who continued to collect original recipes and offering hope after my initial enthusiasm waned. Without these people, this book would not—could not—have been published.

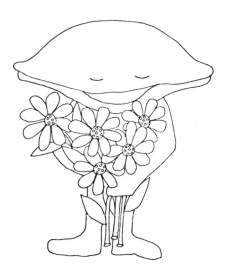

PREFACE TO GORTON'S EDITION

I've known the name "Gorton's of Gloucester" most of my adult life. Gorton's name has always meant seafood of the highest quality.

Much time has been spent in the preparation of this cookbook. I'm happy to be associated with Gorton's in spreading the word that clams are delicious and fun to eat.

William Flagg
Author

PREFACE

When you grow up along the shores of Rhode Island, you learn to eat and love clams at just about the same time that other kids are learning to eat breakfast cereals.

As kids, even before we were allowed to use knives, we would dig clams with our toes, break half the shell with a rock and eat the quahaug (as we knew them) right from the shell. Once we had eaten our fill, we'd haul as many as we could carry back to Mom for chowder or a clam boil.

There was an amusement park—Rocky Point—that we'd get to on special occasions. Would you believe that I looked forward more to their chowder and clam cakes than I did the rides!

As a teenager, clam bakes were an exciting event—an all day affair. Dad and I would arrive at mid-morning and watch the bakemasters begin to lay the bake in a wide hole in the ground.

At lunchtime, we'd sit at long tables outdoors. Pitchers full of steaming hot chowder would come, each with a big serving ladle sticking out of the top. With them would be plates piled high with clam cakes. Everyone would eat twice his fill. I'd even get to have a draft beer! The afternoon was spent swimming, playing baseball, horseshoes or "bocci" (an Italian lawn bowling game).

Toward evening, someone would ring a big bell, and then, back to the tables. It was clam bake time! First would come hot steamed clams, piled high in the center of the table, with dishes of hot clam liquor to wash them off and real melted butter to dip them in. In no time, that pile of clams would be a pile of shells. A little of the remaining butter would be added to the clam broth, along with salt and pepper, to make a clear soup to wash the clams down with. Then would come fish and sausage in soggy wax paper envelopes, potatos, carrots and corn on the cob. I'd get to have another beer. When we had gorged ourselves and had no more room at all, there would be a cheer and out would come a lobster for everyone, even me. To top it off, platters of icy watermelon would be served.

When a little older, I remember days at the beach, moonlight swims and romantic evenings by campfire, eating clam bakes from a large tin container that we had put together ourselves.

As an adult, one travels and begins to see a larger world. As I became more and more interested in cooking, I noted that people all over this world ate clams, in a multitude of wonderful ways.

I began to collect these clam recipes, to experiment with them and hopefully improve on some. This book is the result of those efforts. It is my book—a clam *lover's* cookbook.

PREFACE TO THIRD EDITION

By the time I had finally completed the original manuscript for THE CLAM LOVER'S COOKBOOK, I thought that I had reviewed every recipe in the world containing clams.

Not true! About once a month since that time, I'd spot a new recipe. Or I'd be in a restaurant and be served some chef's tasty new clam creation. Also, friends would either give or send me recipes, together with some clever remark I really needed like "Hey, clam expert, how come this recipe isn't in your book?" Well, naturally, I just clammed up, gratefully received their contributions, and filed them in my own copy of THE CLAM LOVER'S COOKBOOK'

I also noted, as I prepared some of the recipes in the book, that sometimes I was not precisely following my own directions.

Well, just about the time my own copy was bursting with additional recipes which I had collected, my publisher notified me that it was time for another printing of the book.

"Wait," says I! "Would there possibly be time for me to modify a few of the recipes, and maybe add a bonus chapter containing some of the new recipes which I've collected?"

The response was an enthusiastic . . . "Yes!" (Fortunately, my publisher is a clam lover too). So, now we have an expanded and revised edition of THE CLAM LOVER'S COOKBOOK.

I sincerely hope you enjoy every recipe in it!

CONTENTS

In A Supporting Role 115

Bonus Chapter 129

INTRODUCTION

WHAT IS A CLAM?

The clam is a bivalve, gray-white in color, with the technical name of Mercenaria mercenaria. It got its name from the fact that Indians used the shells as wampum.

WHAT ARE THE COMMON TYPES?

On the East Coast, there are two common types: hard shell and soft shell.

The hard shell are known by a variety of names, according to their sizes. The smallest that are legally harvested are between 2" and 2 1/2" in diameter and are called littlenecks. Next larger are cherrystone, 2 1/2" to 3" in diameter. Above 3", they are known as quahaugs (or quahogs). In all sizes, the hard shell variety are called hard shell clams, clams, hard clams or round clams.

The larger clams, being tougher, are popular in chowders, while the smaller littlenecks and cherrystone clams are excellent on the half shell or as Clam Casino.

The soft shell or "steamer" clam is popular for steaming, up to about 2 1/2" in length. Above this size, they are delicious fried or in chowder.

On the West Coast, there are also a variety of popular types. Perhaps the most well-known are the Pizmo clam, from Pizmo Beach in California, and the razer clam. Also found on the West Coast are the butter clams, the littlenecks (which is a different variety from the East Coast hard clam) and the mammoth goeduck (pronounced "gooey-duck").

FRESH AND CANNED CLAMS

A true clam lover must ask him or herself, "Should I use fresh or canned clams"?

During the warmer months, and especially in locations near the water, you can easily enjoy the luxury of fresh clams—either store-bought, or, if you have the inclination, "self-dug."

Canned clams are available all year-round in every state of the union. And, let's face it, canned clams are much easier to use. You don't have to dig them, clean them, shuck them, chop them or refrigerate them. With the long "shelf life" of canned clams you can stock them with your canned goods and have one of my delicious recipes whenever the mood strikes you.

HOW TO DIG CLAMS!

First, some bad news. Clams are much less plentiful along our shores now than they were several years ago. Many have been killed by red tide and other pollutants. Even a given spot along a shore may be safe for quahaug-ing at only certain times of the year. The best thing to do is ask a native, he'll be glad to tell you where it's safe and also where the best "pickin" is.

Clams live in salt water, 6 to 8 inches below the surface of the mud or sand. The best place for non-commercial harvesting is along the shore at low tide.

The equipment is simple; for the men a steel garden rake and a burlap bag. Mom will want a pair of old sneakers and a pair of canvas garden gloves. Kids are tougher; all they need are fingers and wiggly toes.

To use the rake, stand in water about 2 to 3 feet deep, dig down with the rake about 10 inches and pull the mud out of the hole. Put the rake back into the small trench and work the rake into the side closer to you. Gradually pull the rake up through the mud toward you. You can usually feel a scraping sensation if a clam (or stone or broken glass) is present. Remove the clams and put them into the burlap bag. The burlap bag can either be tied to your waist, or allowed to float. Proceed in this fashion, working your rake on the near side of the hole. If you find a spot with some clams, expand your efforts in that area to get as many of that colony as possible. Work quickly, because they will burrow away and disappear if you don't.

Mom and kids can use their toes and fingers to search out the burrowing bivalves. This technique is good in water up to about the bottom of your bathing suit. Any deeper, and you'll have to dive to get any clams you find with your feet.

Professional quahaugers use three principal methods to harvest clams. Most common is power dredging, which requires a large boat and some heavy gear. Two methods can be used from a small boat; tonging and bullraking. Tongs are like oversize corn on the cob pincers, with two steel half-baskets on the end. The tongs are between 10 and 16 feet long. The tonger stands in the boat, spreads the handles apart and pinches them together (see cover illustration). The Bullrake is a heavy steel rake, with a handle 20 to 40 feet long. The bullraker works from a drifting boat, slowly raking over the bottom.

HOW TO BUY FRESH CLAMS

Fresh clams may be purchased at most fish markets and a few supermarkets. Most fish dealers will shuck the clams for you if you request them to.

If you are picking out hard shell clams from the bin yourself, discard any that have cracked shells or are not shut tight. Then, check each one to ascertain that it is alive. This is done by knocking two clams together. If they sound like two stones, they are both good. If you hear a hollow sound, one of the two is bad and should not be selected.

If you are selecting soft shell clams, discard any whose shells are broken and those that don't "spring" back when squeezed slightly.

HOW TO CLEAN CLAMS

As mentioned, clams live in sand and mud, and these impurities get inside the shell.

If you are in a boat or along the shore, hang the clams in a burlap bag in the water for up to 24 hours to allow them to clean themselves.

If you are at home, scrub the clams off well with a stiff brush under cold running water. To remove sand, put them in a sink or large pan of fresh water containing 1/2 cup of salt for each gallon of water. Allow hard shell clams to remain in this bath for about one-half hour. Then, change the salted water and repeat the process twice.

With soft shell clams, make up the same water mixture and then sprinkle a little corn meal on the water. This will help to purge the sand inside the clams. Refrigerate the clams in the brine mixture for at least four hours.

HOW TO SHUCK (OPEN) CLAMS

To shuck soft shell clams, an old knife is best. A sharp knife is not necessary and is hazardous. While holding a well-scrubbed clam with the hinge on the palm of one hand, work the blade inside the clam, along the inside of the shell to sever the muscle. Repeat on the opposite side. Discard the shell, together with the black covering over the "neck" and along the shell and the jelly-like substance inside. Wash in clear water and place in a colander to drain.

To shuck hard shell clams, a knife with a strong, thin, sharp blade is required. Hold each well-scrubbed clam in the palm of one hand with the hinge against the palm. With the knife held in the other hand, force the blade between the shells. Leverage may be gained by wrapping the fingers of the hand holding the clam around the top of the knife blade

and squeezing. Cut around the inside edge to sever the connecting mus-
cles, and twist the knife slightly to open the shell. Once the clam is open,
run the knife around the inside to free all the meat. If they are to be
served on the half shell, twist off one half of the shell and capture the
meat in the remaining half. All of the clam is edible.

If the hard shell clam is not to be eaten raw, there are two easier
methods. In the first, spread well-scrubbed clams on a wire rack above a
baking pan. Bake at 450 degrees for 3 to 5 minutes until the clams open
slightly. Discard any clams that will not open. In the second method,
freeze the clams after they have been scrubbed. Once a clam has been
either frozen or quickly baked, it will allow the knife to enter more
easily.

HOW TO STORE FRESH CLAMS

Fresh clams are perishable. Once taken from the water, or from the ice
at the fish market, they should be kept cold. While cleaning the shells at
home, use cold water. Use cold water to purge them of sand in a brine
bath. Once shucked, keep them either in the refrigerator or frozen.

Clams in the shell may be stored in the refrigerator at 40 degrees for
several days.

Shucked clams, surrounded by ice, in a suitable container will keep
for one week.

Clams may be frozen, either in the shell or shucked. To store shucked
clams, put them in plastic containers and cover the clams with their own
juice. Add water if necessary, because any that are exposed to air may
become discolored. Allow at least 1/2" expansion space. They may be
stored at 0 degrees F for 10 months, or at 5 degrees F for 6 months.

HOW TO MEASURE CLAMS

Either fresh or canned clams may be used for the majority of recipes in
this book.

Unless otherwise noted, whenever a liquid measure is specified (ie.,
1/2 cup clams, minced) the source of the clams is optional.

For those clam dishes served in the shell, usually fresh clams are required. In-the-shell recipes (ie., Clams Casino, Deviled Clams) in which
canned clams may be used, are so noted.

Don't you landlocked clam lovers deprive yourselves of these in-the-
shell dishes because you may not always have access to fresh clams. The
next time you have clams at either a clambake or in a restaurant, save
the shells, boil them to assure cleanliness and use them with canned
clams during the lean periods. Your guests will never know!

Clams are harvested in a variety of sizes and types. During the research for this book, I found that often recipes were misleading, because the cook had specified "two dozen clams." Depending upon the size of the clam used, quite a variance in final results could occur.

In this book, when whole clams are required, the type is also specified. All other recipes specify a liquid measure (ie., 2 cups clams, minced, with liquid). Unless otherwise stated, the natural juices (or liquor) of the clam is also included in the measure.

Canned clams are usually sold in a 6 1/2 ounce size can, and are available in three forms: chopped (3/4" pieces), minced (1/2" pieces) and whole baby clams.

CANNED CLAMS WITH LIQUID

When recipe calls for: *Use:*

1 Cup   1 of the 6 1/2 ounce cans

2 Cups   3 of the 6 1/2 ounce cans

Note: Some canned clams are packed in clam juice, others are packed in water. So read the label. Contents of cans are about 50% clams and 50% juice.

For fresh clams, use the following equation:

1 quart of clams in-the-shell = 2 pounds of clams in-the-shell = 1 cup of shucked clams plus 1 cup of liquid

Following are additional approximate equivalents which may be of help.

Fresh clams	Size	One quart of clams in-the-shell
Hard shells:		
Littleneck	2-2 1/2"	18 - 24
Cherrystone	2 1/2-3"	10 - 14
Quahaug	3"+	4 - 6
Soft shells:		
Steamer	2-2 1/2"	18 - 24
Fry and chowder	2 1/2"+	10 - 18

ABBREVIATIONS USED:

Tsp. = Teaspoon

Tbl. = Tablespoon

As a Beverage

Basic Clam Broth

INGREDIENTS (makes 4 cups)

2	Quarts	Clams in shells
1 3/4	Cups	Water
3	Stalks	Celery with leaves, cut up
1	Pinch	Cayenne pepper

DIRECTIONS

Wash clams and place in pot.

Add remaining ingredients.

Cover the pot and steam clams until shells open.

Strain the liquid through wet double cheesecloth to remove any sand.

Reserve clams for another use.

Use broth in any recipe calling for clam broth, juice or liquid.

Clam Frappe

INGREDIENTS (serves 4)

2	Cups	Clam broth
2 1/2	Cups	Chicken stock or bouillon
		Whipped cream, unsweetened and lightly salted

DIRECTIONS

Mix clam and chicken broths together.

Freeze to mush in an ice cube tray, stirring periodically with a fork.

Place in small prechilled bowls or glasses.

Garnish each serving with a dab of whipped cream.

Serve as a summer first course.

Hot Clam Broth

INGREDIENTS (serves 1)

1	Cup	Clam broth, hot
1	Tsp.	Butter
		Salt
		Pepper

DIRECTIONS

Add butter to hot broth.

Correct seasonings with salt and pepper. Serve hot.

VARIATIONS

Dilute with:
  Chicken broth
  Tomato soup
  V-8 juice
  Consomme
  Warm cream or milk (do not boil again after these additions.)

Top with a spoonful of unsweetened, lightly salted whipped cream.
Sprinkle with chopped chives, parsley, minced, fresh dill or celery salt.

Clam Juice Cocktail

INGREDIENTS (serves 8)

1	Quart	Fresh or canned clam broth, chilled
		Ice cubes

DIRECTIONS

Put two ice cubes in an old fashioned glass.

Fill glass with clam juice.

VARIATIONS

Add a little sherry.
Add a touch of curry powder.
Season with salt, celery salt, a few drops of Tabasco sauce and lemon juice.

Tomato Juice New England

INGREDIENTS (serves 1)

1/2	Cup	Tomato juice
1/2	Cup	Clam juice
1/4	Tsp.	Salt
3	Drops	Tabasco sauce
		Juice from 1/2 lime

DIRECTIONS

Place all ingredients in a blender and blend for 1 minute.

Serve over ice cubes in a chilled glass.

VARIATION

Add 1 or 2 whole cherrystone clams to ingredients in blender.

Bloody Clamdigger

2	Ounces	Clam juice, chilled
2	Ounces	Tomato juice, chilled
2	Ounces	Vodka
2	Tbls.	Lemon juice
		Celery salt
		Ground black pepper
		Worcestershire sauce
		Tabasco sauce
		Celery stick

DIRECTIONS

Put some ice cubes in a tall glass.

Add clam and tomato juices, vodka and lemon juice.

Season to taste with celery salt, pepper, Worcestershire and Tabasco.

Garnish with a stick of crisp celery and serve.

VARIATION

Omit vodka.

Hot Clamato Juice

INGREDIENTS (serves 4)

1	Can	Clamato juice (29 ounces), or 1 can tomato juice (16 ounces) and 2 bottles clam juice (6 ounces)
4	Tbls.	Lemon juice
1/2	Tsp.	Black pepper, freshly ground
1	Tsp.	Celery salt
1	Tsp.	Onion salt
1	Tsp.	Dry mustard
1	Tsp.	Worcestershire sauce
1/2	Tsp.	Tabasco sauce

DIRECTIONS

Combine ingredients in top section of double boiler.

Put 1 inch of water in lower section and heat for 10 minutes.

Serve hot in mugs.

Canapes and Dips

Hot Clam Puffs

INGREDIENTS (makes about 36)

1	Package	Cream cheese (3 ounces), softened
1/4	Tsp.	Dry mustard
1/4	Tsp.	Salt
2	Tbls.	Heavy cream
2	Tsp.	Worcestershire sauce
1/2	Tsp.	Grated onion or onion juice
1/2	Cup	Minced clams, drained
36		Toast rounds, 1" to 2" in diameter
		Paprika

DIRECTIONS

In the order listed, cream together the cheese, mustard, salt, cream, Worcestershire sauce, onion and clams.

Sprinkle with paprika.

Heap mixture on toast rounds.

Place in broiler about 3" from heat for 2 to 3 minutes or until brown.

Sauterne Clam Puffs

INGREDIENTS (makes 20)

1	Package	Cream cheese (8 ounces), softened
1/4	Cup	Sauterne wine
1/2	Cup	Minced clams, drained
20		Toast rounds, 1" to 2" in diameter
3	Strips	Bacon, cut in 1" pieces

DIRECTIONS

Place cheese in a bowl. Blend in wine and clams.

Heap onto toast rounds.

Top with a piece of bacon.

Place in broiler, about 3" from heat, for 5 minutes or until bacon is crisp.

Clam Puffs

INGREDIENTS (makes 24)

1/3	Cup	Mayonnaise
1/2	Tsp.	Horseradish
1/2	Tsp.	Garlic salt
1/2	Cup	Minced clams, drained
1		Egg white
24		Melba rounds

DIRECTIONS

Blend together mayonnaise, horseradish, garlic salt and minced clams.

Beat egg white until stiff and add to clam mixture.

Pile onto melba rounds.

Place in broiler, about 3" from heat, for 2 to 3 minutes, until puffed and brown.

Clam Rafts

INGREDIENTS (makes 6 rafts)

1/2	Cup	Clams, minced and drained
3/4	Cup	Cottage cheese
6	Tbls.	Sour cream
1	Tsp.	Salt
1/4	Tsp.	Pepper
1	Dash	Cayenne pepper
6		Crisp rye wafers
6		Small onion rings
2	Tbls.	Chili sauce

DIRECTIONS

Mix together clams, cottage cheese, sour cream, salt and peppers.

Spread mixture onto rye wafers.

Top each with an onion ring.

Fill each ring with 1 teaspoon chili sauce.

Broil about 5" from heat for 5 to 6 minutes.

Clams Gourmet *

INGREDIENTS (serves 4)

1	Cup	White clam sauce (see recipe in sauce chapter)
8	Ounces	Monterey Jack cheese, shredded
1	Tbl.	Parsley, chopped
1	Tbl.	Chives, chopped
4	Slices	Pumpernickle bread, toasted on one side

DIRECTIONS

Put bread, toasted side down, into individual baking dishes.

Combine clam sauce, cheese, parsley and chives. Spread 1/4 of mixture onto each slice of bread.

Place in broiler, about 3" from heat, for 3 to 4 minutes, until bubbly and beginning to brown.

Compliments of the Dolphin Inn, Buzzards Bay, Massachusetts

Clam Crisps

INGREDIENTS (makes 24)

1	Tbl.	Butter
2	Tbls.	Onions, finely chopped
1 1/2	Tbls.	Flour
1/4	Tsp.	Worcestershire sauce
1/4	Tsp.	Garlic powder
1	Cup	Minced clams
12	Slices	Fresh bread, crusts removed
		Butter

DIRECTIONS

Saute onions in butter until transparent.

Blend in flour.

Add clams, clam liquid, Worcestershire sauce and garlic powder. Cook until mixture thickens and boils, about 1 minute. Set aside and cool.

Flatten each bread slice with a rolling pin and spread with butter.

Spread with clam mixture and roll up, jelly roll fashion. Cut in half.

Secure each roll with a toothpick if necessary.

Place in a well-buttered baking dish. Brush with melted butter.

Bake in a preheated 425 degree oven for 8 to 10 minutes, or until nicely browned.

Serve hot.

Note: These can be made ahead of time and refrigerated or frozen.

Little Clambakes

INGREDIENTS (makes 48)

1	Package	Cream cheese (8 ounces), softened
1/2	Cup	Chopped clams, thoroughly drained
1	Tbl.	Onion, grated
1/2	Tsp.	Tabasco sauce
4	Dozen	Buttery crackers
		Paprika

DIRECTIONS

Blend together cheese, clams, onion and Tabasco sauce. (May be refrigerated at this point.)

Just before serving, spread 1 teaspoonful of clam mixture on each cracker.

Sprinkle lightly with paprika and place on large cookie sheets.

Bake in preheated 400 degree oven for about 5 minutes until heated through, but not browned.

Serve hot, garnished with a slice of black olive or green olive with pimiento.

Clam Balls

INGREDIENTS (makes 24-36 balls, 1" in diameter)

1/4	Cup	Butter, melted
1 1/4	Cups	Ritz crackers, crushed
1	Cup	Clams, minced, with liquid
1	Tbl.	Lemon juice

DIRECTIONS

Mix together all ingredients.

Form into 1" balls and place on cookie sheet.

Bake in preheated 350 degree oven for 15 minutes.

Turn each ball over and bake 5 to 15 minutes longer, until nicely browned.

Serve on toothpicks, plain or with cocktail sauce.

Chafing Dish Clam Canapes

INGREDIENTS (makes about 24)

3	Tbls.	Butter
1/2	Cup	Onions, finely chopped
1/2	Cup	Green bell pepper, finely chopped
1/2	Cup	Minced clams, drained
1/4	Pound	Sharp cheddar cheese, diced
1/4	Cup	Catsup
1	Tbl.	Worcestershire sauce
1	Tbl.	Dry sherry
1/4	Tsp.	Cayenne pepper
3	Drops	Tabasco sauce
24		Melba toast rounds

DIRECTIONS

Melt butter in frying pan.

Saute onions and pepper for 3 minutes, until onion is transparent.

Add clams, cheese, catsup, Worcestershire sauce, sherry, pepper and Tabasco sauce.

Heat until cheese melts.

Adjust seasoning and serve from chafing dish on melba rounds.

Clam Stuffed Mushroom Caps

INGREDIENTS (makes about 36)

1/2	Cup	Butter
2	Pounds	Mushrooms, 1 1/2" to 2" in diameter
1	Cup	Minced clams, with liquid
1	Clove	Garlic, minced
1/2	Cup	Dried bread crumbs
1/3	Cup	Parsley, chopped
3/4	Tsp.	Salt
1/4	Tsp.	Ground black pepper
		Lemon juice

DIRECTIONS

Melt butter in sauce pan.

Remove and dice mushroom stems.

Dip caps in butter and place, rounded side down, on a rack on a cookie sheet.

Drain clams and reserve liquid.

In melted butter, saute mushroom stems and garlic. Add clam liquid and simmer until mushroom stems are tender.

Remove from heat and stir in remaining ingredients.

Spoon mixture into mushroom caps.

Broil about 6" from heat for about 8 minutes, until mushrooms are tender and tops are lightly browned.

Sprinkle a few drops of lemon juice on each and serve hot.

Mushrooms Stuffed With Whole Clams

INGREDIENTS (makes 24)

24		Mushrooms, 2" in diameter
3	Tbls.	Butter, melted
24		Littleneck clams, shucked
5	Tbls.	Horseradish
8	Tbls.	Mayonnaise
1	Tsp.	Worcestershire sauce
6	Drops	Tabasco sauce

DIRECTIONS

Remove stems from mushrooms and reserve for another use.

Wipe mushroom caps with a towel, dip in butter, and place, rounded side down, on a rack on a cookie sheet.

Place 1 clam in each mushroom cap.

Mix together remaining ingredients and spoon over clams.

Broil about 6" from heat for about 8 minutes or until mushrooms are tender and topping begins to brown.

Fried Clam Appetizer

INGREDIENTS (makes 24)

24		Littleneck, cherrystone or steamer clams, scrubbed clean
2	Cups	White wine
1/4	Tsp.	Ground black pepper
1	Cup	Flour
1/4	Tsp.	Salt
1/8	Tsp.	Ground black pepper
2		Eggs, beaten
		Olive oil

DIRECTIONS

Put the clams in a kettle. Add the wine and season with pepper. Cover and steam until clam shells open.

Once all have opened, allow to cool in the liquid. Remove clams and discard shells.*

Blend together flour, salt and pepper.

Dip clams in beaten egg and roll in flour mixture.

Fry in hot olive oil, deep enough to cover clams.

Serve hot on toothpicks, with cocktail sauce and tartar sauce.

*Note: If soft shell steamer clams are used, discard the black covering over the "neck" and along the shell.

Clam Dip—I

INGREDIENTS (makes 2 1/2 cups)

2	Packages	Cream cheese (3 ounces), softened
1	Tbl.	Worcestershire sauce
1	Tbl.	Lemon juice
1	Clove	Garlic, minced (or 1/4 teaspoon garlic powder)
1/2	Tsp.	Salt
1/8	Tsp.	Ground black pepper
1	Tbl.	Horseradish
1/4	Tsp.	Mustard powder
1	Tbl.	Onion, grated
3	Drops	Tabasco sauce
2	Tbls.	Clam juice, from the minced clams
1/2	Cup	Sour cream
1/2	Cup	Minced clams, with liquid reserved
1	Tsp.	Chives, chopped
		Paprika

DIRECTIONS

Place all ingredients through Tabasco sauce in a mixing bowl.

Mix with electric mixer at low speed until thoroughly blended.

Add clam juice and continue mixing.

Add sour cream and mix until mixture is the consistency of whipped cream.

Add clams and blend at low speed.

Add chives and blend only until mixed.

Pour into serving dish and shape top into half ball.

Chill for at least one-half hour.

Sprinkle with paprika.

Garnish with chives, parsley, pimiento, sliced onion or small whole clams.

Serve with saltines or potato chips.

Clam Dip—II

INGREDIENTS (makes 2 cups)

8	Ounces	Cottage cheese
4	Ounces	Cream cheese
1	Envelope	Onion soup mix (1 1/8 ounces)
2	Tsp.	Worcestershire sauce
1/2	Cup	Sour cream
1/2	Cup	Minced clams, drained

DIRECTIONS

At low speed in a mixer, blend together the cottage cheese, cream cheese, onion soup mix, Worcestershire sauce and sour cream.

Add the clams, together with a little clam liquid if necessary to moisten and blend until mixed.

Pour into attractive serving dish and chill.

Serve with potato chips, corn chips or celery sticks.

Hot Clam Dip

INGREDIENTS

1/4	Cup	Green pepper, chopped
1/3	Cup	Onion, chopped
1/4	Cup	Butter
1	Cup	Processed cheese spread, cubed (about 4 ounces)
1	Cup	Clams, minced, with liquid
1/4	Cup	Chili sauce

DIRECTIONS

Saute pepper and onion in butter until onion is soft.

Add cheese and cook over low heat, stirring constantly until cheese is melted.

Add clams and chili sauce. Heat through.

Serve hot with crackers.

Clam Dilly Dip

INGREDIENTS (serves 8)

1	Package	Cream cheese (8 ounces), softened
2	Tbls.	White wine, Reisling
1	Tbl.	Mayonnaise
1/2	Cup	Cooked clams, chopped and drained
3	Tbls.	Dill pickles, chopped
5		Pimiento-stuffed olives, chopped
1/4	Cup	Celery, finely chopped
1/2	Tsp.	Horseradish
1	Tsp.	Soy sauce
1	Tsp.	Onion, grated
1/4	Tsp.	Salt
		Paprika
		Parsley sprigs

DIRECTIONS

Mix cream cheese, wine and mayonnaise until well blended.

Add remaining ingredients through salt and blend well.

Pile into a decorative serving bowl. Sprinkle with paprika and garnish with a few sprigs of parsley.

Serve with potato chips or crackers.

Clams in Crusty Cups

INGREDIENTS (makes 24 appetizers)

12	Slices	White bread
8	Tbls.	Butter (1 stick), melted
5	Tbls.	Butter
2	Tbls.	Flour
1	Cup	Half-and-half
1/8	Tsp.	Salt
1/8	Tsp.	Black pepper, freshly ground
1	Tbls.	Dijon style mustard
4	Tbls.	Grated Parmesan cheese
1/4	Cup	Scallions, minced
2	Cans	Minced clams (6-1/2 ounces each), drained
1	Clove	Garlic, minced
2	Tbls.	Parsley flakes

DIRECTIONS

Make the cups: Roll the bread slices very thin with a rolling pin.
With a 2" cutter, cut out 2 rounds from each slice. Fit the rounds
gently into well buttered 1-1/4" muffin tins (gem tins), being careful
not to tear them. Brush them with about half of the melted butter.
Bake them, in a preheated 375° oven, for 10 to 12 minutes, until
edges are golden. Remove the cups from the tins. Let them cool on
a rack and then arrange them on a baking sheet.

Make the filling: Melt 3 tablespoons of the butter in a saucepan over
medium heat. Add the flour and mix well. Gradually add the half-
and-half. Cook, stirring continuously, until a smooth sauce has
formed. Add salt and pepper. Cook sauce for about 10 minutes.
Remove from heat and stir in the mustard and 2 tablespoons of the
Parmesan cheese.

Melt the remaining 2 tablespoons of butter in a skillet. Add the
Scallions and saute until softened. Add the clams and the garlic.
Cook, while stirring, for about 3 minutes. Stir this mixture into the
sauce. Add the parsley and adjust the seasonings.

Spoon the resulting mixture into the cups. Sprinkle them with the
remaining Parmesan cheese and drizzle them with the remaining
butter. Broil, about 6" from the heat source, for about 5 minutes,
until they are golden and the filling is bubbly.

In the Shell

Clams on the Half Shell

INGREDIENTS (serves 6 as a first course)

36   Littleneck or cherrystone clams
       Crushed ice
       Cocktail sauce
       Lemon wedges

DIRECTIONS

Clean the clams. Open the shells, pry the clam meat loose. Discard the top shells.

Arrange 6 clams on a bed of crushed ice in each of 6 shallow bowls or plates.

Place a small container of cocktail sauce in the center of each dish.

Garnish with lemon wedges.

Cocktail Sauce

INGREDIENTS

1/2	Cup	Catsup
1	Tbl.	Lemon juice
1	Tbl.	Horseradish
3	Drops	Tabasco sauce
1/2	Tsp.	Celery salt
1/4	Tsp.	Salt

DIRECTIONS

Blend all ingredients.

Chill.

Roast Clams

INGREDIENTS (serves 6 as a main course, 12 as an appetizer)

6   Quarts   Littleneck or cherrystone clams
                 Butter

DIRECTIONS

Scrub clams thoroughly.

When indoors:

   Place in baking dish.

   Roast in 450 degree oven for 5 minutes or just until clams open.

When cooking out:

   Place clams on grid over hot coals until clams are hot and open.

Twist off top shell with gloves or oven mitts.

Add a little butter and serve hot in their shells.

Clams Casino

INGREDIENTS (serves 6)

		Rock salt
24		Littleneck or cherrystone clams
1/2	Cup	Butter
1/4	Cup	Onion, finely diced
1/4	Cup	Green bell pepper, finely diced
1	Clove	Garlic, minced
1/4	Tsp.	Salt
1/4	Tsp.	Ground black pepper
1/8	Tsp.	Ground cayenne pepper (optional)
3/4	Cup	Bread crumbs
3	Tbls.	Parsley, chopped
1	Tbl.	Lemon juice
3	Strips	Bacon, cut into 1" pieces

DIRECTIONS

Place rock salt 1/2" deep in the bottom of a shallow baking pan.

Scrub the clams thoroughly. Open them and discard half the shell. Cut clam into quarters and place in bottom half of shell. Settle clam shells in the bed of rock salt. This will keep them from tipping and losing their juices during cooking.

Melt butter in a frying pan.

Saute onion, garlic and pepper until onions are transparent.

Remove from heat and add salt, black and cayenne peppers, bread crumbs, parsley and lemon juice.

Mix together lightly and spoon onto the tops of the clams.

Top each one with a piece of bacon.

Bake in a preheated 500 degree oven for 5 minutes or until hot.

Place pan about 3" from heat under the broiler for 1 minute or until bacon is crisp.

Serve hot with lemon wedges on a bed of hot rock salt.

Venetian Style Stuffed Clams

INGREDIENTS (serves 4)

1/3	Cup	Butter, softened
2	Tbls.	Shallots, chopped
3	Tbls.	Parsley, chopped
1	Tbl.	Chives, chopped
1	Tbl.	Chervil, chopped
4	Drops	Tabasco sauce
1/4	Tsp.	Salt
1/8	Tsp.	Pepper
24		Littleneck or cherrystone clams, well scrubbed
		Rock salt

DIRECTIONS

Cream together the butter, shallots, parsley, chives, chervil, Tabasco sauce, salt and pepper.

Open the clams and discard half the shell. Cut clam into halves or quarters and place in bottom of shell.

Cover each clam with the butter mixture.

Place rock salt 1/2" deep in the bottom of a shallow baking pan. Place in preheated 500 degree oven until hot, about 5 minutes.

Remove rock salt from oven and settle clams in the bed of rock salt.

Broil for 5 to 6 minutes about 5" from heat.

Serve hot with lemon wedges.

Deviled Clams

INGREDIENTS (makes 6 appetizers)

6		Large clams, about 3" to 4" across
1/4	Cup	Butter
1	Clove	Garlic, minced
1/2	Cup	Onion, chopped
1/3	Cup	Green bell pepper, chopped
1/3	Cup	Celery, chopped
1/2	Cup	Cracker crumbs
1/2	Cup	Bread crumbs
2	Tbls.	Parsley, chopped
3/4	Tsp.	Salt
1/4	Tsp.	Black pepper, ground
1/8	Tsp.	Cayenne pepper, ground
1/4	Tsp.	Monosodium glutamate (MSG or Accent)
3	Drops	Tabasco sauce
2	Tsp.	Prepared mustard
1/2	Tsp.	Thyme
1		Egg, beaten

DIRECTIONS

Scrub and shuck clams. Save the shells.

Drain and chop clams. Save the clam liquid.

Melt butter in a frying pan.

Saute onion, garlic, pepper and celery until onion is transparent.

Add clams with liquid and simmer over low heat for 5 minutes.

Remove from heat, add remaining ingredients and mix together.

Fill half of the shells with this mixture.

Bake in 350 degree oven for about 30 minutes, or until tops are nicely browned.

Serve very hot with a lemon wedge.

Baked Clams

INGREDIENTS (makes 6 appetizers)

6		Clams, 3" to 4" across
1 1/2	Cups	White bread, diced
1/3	Cup	Milk
1/3	Cup	Butter, melted
1/4	Cup	Water chestnuts, diced
4	Tsp.	Soy sauce
2	Slices	Bacon, cooked and crumbled
1/4	Tsp.	Ginger, powdered
1/4	Cup	Scallions, chopped
1	Tbl.	Parsley, chopped
1/2	Tsp.	Black pepper
1	Tbl.	Sesame seed
1/3	Cup	Parmesan cheese, grated
1/4	Cup	Butter, melted
		Paprika

DIRECTIONS

Scrub and shuck the clams. Save the shells.

Chop clams. Save the clam liquid.

Moisten the bread crumbs with milk.

Mix together the clams, clam juice, bread with milk, butter, water chestnuts, soy sauce, bacon, ginger, scallions, parsley and pepper.

Fill half of the clam shells with this mixture.

Sprinkle with sesame seed, cheese, butter and paprika.

Bake in preheated 375 degree oven for about 10 minutes, until hot and nicely browned.

Serve hot with cocktail sauce.

Clams St. Jacques

INGREDIENTS (makes 4)

16		Littleneck or small steamer clams, well scrubbed
3/4	Cup	Dry white wine
1	Clove	Garlic, minced
1	Tbl.	Parsley, chopped
1	Stalk	Celery, chopped
2	Tbls.	Butter
2	Tbls.	Flour
1/8	Tsp.	Salt
1/8	Tsp.	Black pepper
1	Dash	Cayenne pepper
1	Tbl.	Parsley, chopped
1/4	Cup	Gruyere cheese, grated
1/4	Cup	Bread crumbs
1/8	Stick	Butter

DIRECTIONS

Place clams, wine, garlic, parsley and celery in saucepan. Simmer gently for 5 minutes, until clam shells open.

Strain the liquid through wet double cheesecloth to remove the flavoring ingredients, as well as any sand.

Remove the clams from the shells. Discard the shells. If steamer clams are used, also discard the black covering from the "neck" and along the shell.

Melt the butter in a saucepan. Add the flour and stir until a paste forms. Gradually add 1 cup of clam liquid, stirring constantly, until a smooth white sauce has been made.

Add the salt, pepper, cayenne, parsley, cheese and clams. Heat just to a simmer and remove from stove. Taste and adjust seasonings.

Divide mixture among 4 scallop shells or ramekins. Sprinkle with bread crumbs and dot with pieces of butter.

Bake in a preheated 375 degree oven for 8 to 10 minutes, until lightly browned.

Serve hot.

Clams Farcis

INGREDIENTS (serves 4)

2	Dozen	Cherrystone clams
1	Cup	Milk
2	Slices	Onion, thin
1		Whole clove
5	Tbls.	Butter
3	Tbls.	Flour
1/4	Pound	Mushrooms, cleaned and finely chopped
		Salt
		Black pepper, freshly ground
		Bread crumbs
		Rock salt

DIRECTIONS

Open the clams, retaining any available juice. Reserve the 24 largest half shells. Finely chop the clams.

Heat the milk in a saucepan, together with the onion and clove, for about 5 minutes. Do not allow to boil. Discard the onion and clove.

Heat 3 tablespoons of butter in a skillet. Blend in flour. While stirring, gradually add the clam juice and the milk. Stir until smooth and remove from heat.

Heat remaining butter in another skillet and saute mushrooms until moisture just disappears.

Combine the chopped clams and the mushrooms with the sauce. Season to taste with salt and pepper.

Spoon the mixture into the reserved clam shells and sprinkle with bread crumbs.

Place on rock salt in individual baking dishes and bake in a preheated 450 degree oven for 4 to 5 minutes, until the sauce bubbles.

Spicey Stuffed Clams

INGREDIENTS (serves 4)

12	Large	Hard shell clams, 3" to 4" across
2	Tbls.	Olive oil
3	Tbls.	Butter
1	Cup	Onion, chopped fine
1	Tsp.	Dried thyme
1	Tsp.	Chopped chives
1/4	Tsp.	Crushed dried red pepper flakes
4	Slices	Whole wheat bread, crusts removed and bread cut into 1/4" dice
6	Tbls.	Half-and-half or light cream
3	Tbls.	Grated Parmesan cheese
3	Tbls.	Parsley flakes

DIRECTIONS

Scrub and shuck the clams. Save the juice and 12 of the shells. Chop the clams coarsely and again save the juice.

Heat the olive oil and butter in a skillet over medium heat. Add the onion, thyme, chives and red pepper flakes. Saute for about 3 minutes, stirring constantly, until the onion is transparent.

Add the chopped clams (no liquid at this time) and again saute for about 3 minutes, stirring frequently. Fold in the diced bread, and toss everything together. Saute for another 3 minutes.

Remove skillet from heat and add just enough of the reserved clam juice to moisten.

Fill the 12 reserved clam shells with this mixture, dividing it equally. Carefully spoon about 1-1/2 teaspoons of half-and-half over each. Sprinkle each with Parmesan cheese and parsley. Arrange the stuffed clams on a baking sheet.

Bake, in a preheated 400° oven, for about 5 minutes. Turn off the heat and allow the clams to remain in the oven for another 2 minutes, until lightly browned. Serve very hot.

Salads

Clam Mousse

INGREDIENTS (serves 6)

2	Cups	Clams, chopped, with liquid
2	Tbls.	Unflavored gelatin (2 envelopes)
2	Tbls.	Cold water
1/4	Cup	Dry white wine
1	Cup	Frozen peas, thawed and drained
1	Tbl.	Parsley, finely chopped
1	Tbl.	Chives, coarsely chopped
1		Carrot, peeled and finely chopped
1	Tbl.	Pimiento, minced
2	Stalks	Celery, finely chopped
3/4	Tsp.	Salt
1/4	Tsp.	Pepper, freshly ground
1	Cup	Mayonnaise
1	Cup	Heavy cream, whipped
		Parsley, watercress, ripe olives and/or cherry tomatos for garnish

DIRECTIONS

Drain clams and retain 1/4 cup of liquid for this recipe.

Oil a 2 quart decorative mold or bowl.

In a saucepan, dissolve gelatin in water.

Add wine, clams and clam liquid.·

Cook over low heat, stirring constantly, until gelatin is completely dissolved and clear, about 3 minutes.

Remove from heat, add and mix all remaining ingredients except cream.

Fold in cream and transfer to mold.

Refrigerate about 3 hours until firm.

Unmold and garnish as desired. Clam shells may be used to ring the mold.

Serve with garlic bread and a mixed green salad vinaigrette.

Dilled Clam and Tomato Aspic

INGREDIENTS (serves 6)

2	Bottles	Clam juice (8 ounces)
2	Tsp.	Dill seed
2	Packages	Unflavored gelatin
1	Can	Tomato juice (18 ounces)
2	Tbls.	Scallions, diced
1	Package	Frozen mixed vegetables or peas (10 ounces), cooked, drained and chilled

DIRECTIONS

Combine one bottle of clam juice and the dill seed in a small saucepan. Bring to a boil and simmer for 10 minutes. Using a small sieve, strain seed from clam juice and discard.

Soften gelatin in remaining bottle of clam juice.

Add hot clam juice to gelatin and stir until dissolved.

Add tomato juice and stir.

Chill until mixture is the consistency of unbeaten egg whites.

Add chilled vegetables and scallion. Spoon into 1 1/2 quart mold.

Chill until firm. Unmold.

Serve on lettuce leaves.

Clam and Potato Salad

INGREDIENTS (serves 4)

2	Tbls.	Butter
1	Cup	Clams, drained and chopped
1	Cup	Cooked potatoes, peeled and diced
2		Hard boiled eggs, chopped
1/2	Cup	Celery, chopped
1/2	Cup	Onion, chopped
2	Tbls.	Pimiento, chopped
1	Tsp.	Salt
1/4	Tsp.	Pepper, freshly ground
1/4	Tsp.	Thyme
1/2	Cup	Mayonnaise

DIRECTIONS

Melt butter in frying pan.

Add clams and saute for 3 minutes.

Combine all ingredients and mix.

Adjust seasoning and chill.

Serve on crisp lettuce leaves.

Seafood Salad

INGREDIENTS (serves 8)

1	Tbl.	Butter
1/2	Cup	Clams, chopped and drained
1/2	Cup	Medium shrimp, peeled and deveined
2	Cans	Chunk-style tuna (7 ounces), drained
1	Cup	Celery, thinly sliced
1/2	Cup	Green onion, finely diced
1/4	Cup	Pimiento, chopped and drained
1/2	Cup	Mayonnaise
1/2	Cup	Dairy sour cream
1	Tbl.	Lemon juice
1	Tsp.	Salt
1/4	Tsp.	Pepper, freshly ground
3		Hard boiled eggs, quartered
1/4	Tsp.	Dillweed, finely chopped

DIRECTIONS

Melt butter in a frying pan.

Saute clams and shrimp for about 3 minutes.

Mix together mayonnaise, sour cream and lemon juice. Beat until smooth.

Add clams, shrimp, tuna, celery, onion, pimiento, salt and pepper.

Toss lightly and chill.

Garnish with eggs and dillweed.

Bisques and
Chowders

Clam Bisque—I

INGREDIENTS (serves 4)

3	Tbls.	Butter
1	Cup	Celery, diced
1/4	Cup	Scallions, diced
3	Tbls.	Flour
1	Quart	Milk
2	Cups	Minced clams, with liquid
1/2	Tsp.	Salt
1	Tsp.	Black pepper, freshly ground
1	Dash	Paprika

DIRECTIONS

Melt butter in a saucepan.

Add celery and scallions. Saute slowly until celery is soft.

Add flour and stir until a paste forms.

Gradually add 3 cups of milk, a little at a time, while continually stirring, until a smooth white sauce has been made.

Add the clams, reserved liquid, salt and pepper.

Heat just to a simmer, then remove from stove and cool for 5 minutes.

Pour into blender. Cover and blend until smooth.

Pour from blender back into saucepan and heat just to a simmer.

Thin as required with the remaining milk.

Correct seasoning and serve, garnished with paprika.

Clam Bisque—II

INGREDIENTS (serves 4 to 6)

2	Cups	Clams, with liquid
2	Cups	Heavy cream
1/2	Tsp.	Salt
3	Drops	Tabasco sauce
		Parsley, finely chopped

DIRECTIONS

Place undrained clams in blender and blend for 30 seconds.

Transfer to the top of a double-boiler and add cream, salt and Tabasco.

Cook over boiling water until mixture just reaches the boiling point.

Serve in hot cups, garnished with a sprinkle of parsley.

VARIATIONS

Just before serving, add 2 tablespoons of cognac or 3 tablespoons of sherry to each cup.

Quick Clam and Mushroom Bisque

INGREDIENTS (serves 2)

1	Cup	Clams, minced, with liquid
1	Can	Condensed cream of mushroom soup (12 ounces)
1/4	Cup	Onion, sliced
1/8	Tsp.	Black pepper, freshly ground
1 1/2	Cups	Milk or cream
		Paprika or finely chopped parsley

DIRECTIONS

Put all ingredients through pepper into a blender.

Cover and blend until smooth.

Pour into a saucepan, add milk and heat to just a simmer. Barely simmer for 2 minutes.

Adjust seasoning and serve, garnished with paprika or parsley.

Clam and Mushroom Bisque

INGREDIENTS (serves 4)

2	Tbls.	Butter
1/2	Pound	Mushrooms, chopped
1/2	Cup	Onion, minced
2	Tbls.	Flour
2	Cups	Clams, minced, with liquid
2	Cups	Cream
1/4	Tsp.	Salt
1/4	Tsp.	Pepper
1/8	Tsp.	Celery salt
		Parsley or chives, finely chopped

DIRECTIONS

Melt butter in saucepan.

Add mushrooms and onions. Saute slowly for 10 minutes.

Add flour and stir.

Gradually add the clam liquid, stirring constantly.

Add the clams and simmer for 5 minutes.

Add the cream and heat just to a simmer. Remove from heat and cool for 5 minutes.

Add salt, pepper and celery salt.

Pour into blender. Cover and blend until smooth.

Pour back into saucepan and heat just to a simmer.

Adjust seasoning and serve, garnished with finely chopped parsley or chives.

Clam and Tomato Bisque

INGREDIENTS (serves 4 to 6)

3	Tbls.	Butter (bacon fat may be substituted for half the butter)
2/3	Cup	Onion, diced
1/2	Cup	Celery, diced
2	Tsp.	Green bell pepper, diced
1	Clove	Garlic, minced
3	Tbls.	Flour
2	Cups	Clams, minced, with liquid
1/2	Tsp.	Salt
1/4	Tsp.	Black pepper, freshly ground
1/4	Tsp.	Dried thyme
1/8	Tsp.	Cayenne pepper
1	Tsp.	Parsley, finely chopped
2	Cups	Stewed tomatos
2	Cups	Milk or cream
		Parsley, finely diced

DIRECTIONS

Melt butter in saucepan.

Saute the onion, celery, pepper and garlic for 5 minutes.

Add flour and stir.

Gradually add clam liquid and then clams, stirring constantly. Simmer for 5 minutes.

Add salt, pepper, thyme, cayenne pepper, parsley and tomatos. Simmer for 5 minutes.

Allow to cool for 5 minutes and then pour into blender. Cover and blend until smooth.

Pour back into saucepan, add milk and reheat just to a simmer.

Adjust seasoning and serve, garnished with parsley.

Minced Clam Bisque

INGREDIENTS (serves 6)

2	Cups	Clams, minced, with liquid
2	Cups	Potatoes, peeled and chopped
1/2	Cup	Onion, peeled and chopped
1		Bay leaf
1	Quart	Milk, scalded
1/4	Tsp.	Salt
1/8	Tsp.	Pepper
1		Whole clove
1/8	Tsp.	Nutmeg
1/2	Cup	Heavy cream, heated
2	Tbls.	Butter
1	Tsp.	Parsley, chopped

DIRECTIONS

Drain clams and reserve liquid.

Place potatoes, onion, clam liquid and bay leaf in saucepan. Cook until potatoes are tender.

Add milk, salt, pepper, clove and nutmeg. Bring quickly to a boil. Remove from heat. Remove bay leaf and clove, discard.

Pour into blender. Cover and blend until smooth.

Pour back into saucepan. Add minced clams and cream. Heat slowly, stirring constantly, but do not allow to boil.

Just before serving, stir in butter.

Garnish with sprinkle of parsley.

Corn and Clam Bisque

INGREDIENTS (serves 6)

2	Cups	Clams, with liquid
1	Can	Whole kernel corn (12 ounces)
1		Small white onion, sliced
2	Cups	Heavy cream
1/2	Tsp.	Salt
1/2	Tsp.	Black pepper, freshly ground
		Pimiento, finely diced

DIRECTIONS

Place the clams, corn and onion in a blender and blend 1 minute.

Transfer to the upper part of a double-boiler and add the cream, salt and pepper.

Heat over hot water until the mixture just reaches the boiling point.

Serve in heated cups with a garnish of diced pimiento.

VARIATION

Add 1/3 cup of bourbon to the hot bisque just before serving.

Manhattan Clam Chowder

INGREDIENTS (serves 4)

1	Tbl.	Butter
1	Cube	Fat salt pork, 1/2" square. diced (2 slices of bacon may be substituted)
2/3	Cup	Onion, diced
1/2	Cup	Celery, diced
2	Tsp.	Green bell pepper, finely minced
1	Clove	Garlic, finely minced
1	Cup	Potatoes, peeled and cubed
1	Tsp.	Salt
1/4	Tsp.	Black pepper, freshly ground
1		Bay leaf
2	Cups	Boiling water
2	Cups	Tomatoes, stewed or canned
1	Tbl.	Catsup
2	Cups	Clams, chopped fine, with liquid
1/4	Tsp.	Dried thyme
1/8	Tsp.	Cayenne pepper
1	Tsp.	Parsley, minced

DIRECTIONS

Melt butter and slowly fry the salt pork in a dutch oven until the fat melts and the pork is crisp and golden. Remove pork bits and save.

Add the onion, celery, bell pepper and garlic. Saute until onion is transparent.

Add potatoes, salt, pepper, bay leaf and boiling water. Simmer for 10 minutes.

Add tomatoes and catsup. Simmer until potatoes are soft.

Add clams, thyme, cayenne pepper, parsley and pork bits.

Simmer 3 minutes. Remove bay leaf. Adjust seasoning and serve.

HINT: If possible, prepare chowder the day before intended use. It improves with age!

VARIATION

When adding the clams, also add 2 cups of cooked, flaked whitefish.

Rhode Island Quahaug Chowder

INGREDIENTS

4	Cups	Quahaugs, with liquid
1 1/2"	Cube	Salt pork, diced (4 slices of diced bacon may be substituted)
1	Cup	Onion, finely diced
3	Cups	Potatoes, peeled and cut into 1/4" cubes.
		Boiling water
1 1/2	Cans	Tomato soup concentrate (12 ounces)
		Salt
		Pepper

DIRECTIONS

Drain clams and reserve liquid. Grind the clams with a food chopper.

Slowly fry the salt pork in a dutch oven until the fat melts and the pork is crisp and golden. Remove pork bits and save.

Add the onion and saute until transparent.

Add potatoes and clam liquid. Add enough boiling water to cover and simmer until fork tender, about 10 minutes.

Add clams and simmer for 2 minutes.

Add tomato soup and bring to a simmer. Remove from heat.

Add back the pork bits.*

Add salt and pepper to taste.

This may be served now or cooled and refrigerated until ready to use. It will taste even better the next day.

*HINT: Instead of adding back the pork bits, save them in a separate container until ready to use. Just before serving the chowder, place the pork bits on a pan in a preheated 400 degreee oven until hot. Spoon over the chowder and serve as they sizzle.

New England Clam Chowder

INGREDIENTS (serves 4)

1/4	Pound	Salt pork (or bacon), diced
1	Medium	Onion, diced (about 1/2 cup)
1-1/2	Cups	Potatoes, peeled and cut into 1/2" cubes
2	Cups	Clam broth
1/2	Tsp.	Salt
1/4	Tsp.	Black pepper, freshly ground
2	Cups	Milk (good), light cream or half-and-half (better), or heavy cream (best)
2	Cups	Clams, drained and chopped fine
3	Tbls.	Butter

DIRECTIONS

In a Dutch oven, cook the salt pork over medium heat until fat has been rendered. With a slotted spoon, remove the bits of pork and reserve. Add the onion. Cook, stirring frequently, until onion is transparent, about 5 minutes.

Add potatoes, clam broth, salt and pepper. Simmer until potatoes are tender but not mushy, about 15 minutes.

Add clams and simmer for 5 minutes.

Add milk, butter and reserved salt pork pieces. Heat, but do not allow to boil after milk has been added. Adjust seasonings as required.

Serve hot with saltines.

NOTE: This chowder may be served immediately, or refrigerated and served the next day. Like most stews and chowders, it seems to improve with age.

VARIATION: Just before serving the chowder, place the bits of salt pork onto a baking sheet. Bake, in a preheated 400° oven, for about 5 minutes, until they are hot and crispy. Ladle chowder into serving cups or bowls, and sprinkle the hot bits of pork on top as a garnish.

Martha's Vineyard Quahaug Stew

INGREDIENTS (serves 6 to 8)

1/2	Cup	Butter
2	Tbls.	Flour
4	Cups	Milk
1/4	Tsp.	Salt
1/8	Tsp.	Black pepper, freshly ground
1/8	Tsp.	Mace
1	Quart	Quahaugs, shucked, coarsely chopped, with liquid
2		Eggs, well beaten

DIRECTIONS

Melt butter in a saucepan over low heat.

Add flour and stir until smooth.

Stir in the milk, salt, pepper and mace.

Heat the mixture but do not allow to boil.

In separate saucepan heat clam liquid to a simmer. Skim off froth. Add clams and simmer for 3 minutes. Stir clams and broth into heated milk.

Put eggs into soup tureen. Pour in quahaug mixture, stir well and serve.

Gourmet Clam Soup

INGREDIENTS (serves 2)

6	Tbls.	Butter
1	Tbl.	Scallions, white part only, finely chopped
1	Clove	Garlic, finely chopped
2	Tbls.	Chives, finely chopped
1	Tsp.	White pepper, ground
3/4	Cup	Dry white wine
1/2	Cup	Clam juice
2	Tbls.	Lemon juice
2	Dozen	Cherrystone or littleneck clams, well scrubbed
1/2	Tsp.	Salt

DIRECTIONS

Melt the butter in a large skillet. Do not allow butter to brown.

Add scallions and garlic. Saute lightly for a few seconds.

Add chives, pepper, wine, clam and lemon juices and the clams.

Cover and simmer gently for 10 minutes, until clam shells open. Discard any that do not open.

Taste, and if necessary, adjust seasoning with salt.

Place 12 clams per person in soup bowls. Spoon over the remaining liquid from the pan.

Provide both a soup spoon and a small fork for the clams.

Wild Onion and Clam Chowder

INGREDIENTS (serves 6 to 8)

4	Tbls.	Butter
1	Cup	Wild onions (or scallions or green onions), chopped
1	Cup	Onion, chopped
4	Tbls.	Flour
1	Quart	Milk
2	Cups	Clams, minced, with liquid
1	Tsp.	Salt
1/8	Tsp.	Black pepper, ground
1	Dash	Celery salt

DIRECTIONS

Saute wild onion and onion in butter for 5 minutes.

Add flour and stir until blended.

Gradually add milk, while stirring.

Heat to just below boiling while stirring constantly.

Add clams, salt, pepper and celery salt.

Simmer uncovered for 10 minutes.

Quick Clam Chowder

INGREDIENTS (serves 2)

1	Cup	Clams, minced, with juice
1	Cup	Water
1	Cup	Light cream
1	Tbl.	Sherry (or to taste)

DIRECTIONS

Heat clams, clam juice and water in saucepan and simmer for 1 minute.

Lower heat and add cream, stirring to make sure it doesn't curdle.

Add the sherry, taste for flavor and serve.

Clam Chowder Base, For:

INGREDIENTS (makes 2 quarts of base)

1	Tbl.	Butter
2"	Cube	Salt pork, diced (4 slices of diced bacon may be substituted)
1	Cup	Onion, diced
1/2	Cup	Celery, diced
3	Cups	Potatoes, peeled and cut into 1/4" cubes.
2	Tsp.	Salt
1/2	Tsp.	Black pepper
2	Cups	Boiling water
3	Cups	Clams, chopped, with liquid

DIRECTIONS

Melt butter and slowly fry the salt pork in a dutch oven, until the fat melts and the pork is crisp and golden. Remove pork bits and save.

Add the onion and celery. Saute until onion is transparent.

Add potatoes, salt, pepper and clam liquid. Add boiling water and simmer for 10 minutes.

Add clams and simmer for 3 minutes.

Allow to cool, mix in the pork bits and refrigerate until ready to use. This base will keep for one week at 40 degrees F under refrigeration.

Natural Clam Chowder

INGREDIENTS (serves 4 to 6)

4	Cups	Clam chowder base
2	Cups	Water
1/4	Tsp.	Dried thyme
1/4	Tsp.	Celery salt

DIRECTIONS

Place chowder base, water, thyme and celery salt in a large saucepan and simmer slowly for 5 minutes.

Adjust seasonings and serve.

VARIATION

Use chicken stock instead of water.

Rhode Island Quahaug Chowder

INGREDIENTS (serves 4 to 6)

4	Cups	Clam chowder base
1	Can	Whole tomatoes (16 ounces), cut into small pieces

DIRECTIONS

Place chowder base and tomatoes in a large saucepan and simmer slowly for 5 minutes.

Adjust seasonings and serve.

New England Clam Chowder

INGREDIENTS (serves 4 to 6)

4	Cups	Clam chowder base
2	Cups	Milk or light cream
3	Tbls.	Butter
1	Tsp.	Parsley, chopped

DIRECTIONS

Place the chowder base in a large saucepan and simmer slowly for 5 minutes.

Add the milk and butter. Heat but do not allow to boil.

Adjust seasoning and serve, sprinkled with a little parsley.

Manhattan Clam Chowder

INGREDIENTS (serves 4 to 6)

2	Cups	Tomatos, stewed or canned
1	Tsp.	Catsup
1	Tbl.	Green bell pepper, minced
1/8	Tsp.	Cayenne pepper, ground
1	Clove	Garlic, finely minced
1		Bay leaf
1/4	Tsp.	Dried thyme
1	Tsp.	Parsley, minced
4	Cups	Clam chowder base

DIRECTIONS

Mix the tomatos, catsup, bell pepper, garlic, bay leaf, thyme, cayenne pepper and parsley in a large saucepan and simmer slowly for 15 minutes. Remove bay leaf and discard.

Add the chowder base, heat up again, and simmer slowly for 5 minutes.

Adjust seasonings and serve.

Maryland Clam Chowder

INGREDIENTS (serves 4 to 6)

2	Cups	Chicken stock
1		Chicken breast, skinned, boned and diced
1/2	Cup	Carrots, peeled and diced
1	Clove	Garlic, finely minced
1/4	Tsp.	Celery salt
1/4	Tsp.	Dried thyme
1	Cup	Corn niblets
1	Cup	Peas, frozen
1		Pimiento, chopped fine
4	Cups	Clam chowder base
1/4	Tsp.	Salt
1/8	Tsp.	Pepper

DIRECTIONS

Place chicken stock, breast, carrots, garlic, celery salt and thyme in a large saucepan and simmer for 20 minutes.

Add corn, peas, pimiento, chowder base, chives, salt and pepper. Simmer for 5 minutes.

Adjust seasonings and serve.

Clam Stew—I

INGREDIENTS (serves 4)

2	Tbls.	Butter
1		2" onion, coarsely chopped
2	Ribs	Celery, with tops, cut in 1/2" slices
1 1/2	Cups	Potatoes, peeled and cut into 1/2" cubes
2		Carrots, peeled and cut into 1/2" slices
1 1/2	Cups	Chicken stock, hot
1/2	Tsp.	Salt
1/8	Tsp.	Pepper
2	Cups	Clams, minced, with liquid
1	Cup	Nonfat dry milk powder
		Paprika

DIRECTIONS

Heat butter in large saucepan. Add onion and celery. Saute until onion is transparent.

Add potatoes, carrots, hot chicken stock, salt and pepper. Simmer for 20 minutes, until potatoes and carrots are tender.

Add clams and milk powder. Simmer slowly for 5 minutes. Do not allow to boil.

Adjust seasonings and serve, sprinkled with paprika.

NOTE: This should be thick, but you may wish to add more liquid.

Clam Stew—II

INGREDIENTS (serves 8 to 10)

4		Carrots, peeled and diced
1	Cup	Peas, fresh or frozen
6		New potatoes, 2", peeled and diced
6		White onions, 1 1/2", peeled
4	Stalks	Celery, scraped and sliced
1	Can	Cream style corn (8 3/4 ounces)
2		Bay leaves
1/4	Tsp.	Basil
1/4	Tsp.	Rosemary
1/4	Tsp.	Thyme
1/4	Tsp.	Black pepper, ground
2	Cups	Clam juice
2	Cups	Clams, minced and drained
1	Cup	Butter
10	Rounds	French bread, 1" thick, toasted

DIRECTIONS

Put all ingredients through clam juice in a kettle or dutch oven. Add water to barely cover vegetables.

Bring to boil and simmer, covered, until all vegetables are tender. Remove bay leaves and discard.

Add clams and butter. Simmer for 3 minutes. Adjust seasonings.

Place in serving dish and serve topped with bread rounds.

Traditional Clam Stew

INGREDIENTS (serves 4)

1/4	Cup	Butter
2	Dozen	Littleneck or small soft shell steamer clams, shucked, with liquid
1	Tbl.	Worcestershire sauce
1	Tsp.	Celery salt
1/8	Tsp.	Black pepper, freshly ground
1/4	Tsp.	Paprika
1	Quart	Milk

DIRECTIONS

Heat butter in large saucepan. Add clams, Worcestershire sauce, celery salt and pepper. Saute for 2 minutes, stirring constantly.

Add milk and reheat quickly. Do not boil.

Adjust seasoning and serve with a sprinkle of paprika and a lump of butter on top.

Pass saltines or oyster crackers.

Vatapa

INGREDIENTS (serves 6 to 8)

4	Cups	Manhattan clam chowder (see recipe)
1		Beef bouillon cube
1/2	Cup	Salted peanuts, chopped
1/4	Cup	Coconut, shredded
3	Drops	Tabasco sauce
1	Pound	Shrimp, peeled and deveined

DIRECTIONS

Combine all ingredients, except shrimp, and bring to a boil, stirring frequently.

Add shrimp, simmer for 5 minutes and serve.

Patties, Fritters and Cakes

Light and Fluffy Clam Cakes

INGREDIENTS (makes about 24 cakes, 2" in diameter)

2	Cups	Clams, minced, with liquid
2		Eggs
1/2	Cup	Milk
1 1/2	Cups	All purpose flour
2	Tsp.	Baking powder
1/2	Tsp.	Salt
1/8	Tsp.	Pepper
1	Dash	Cayenne pepper
1/2	Tsp.	Parsley flakes or chopped chives
		Shortening or salad oil for deep frying

DIRECTIONS

Drain clams and reserve liquid.

Beat eggs until light in a large mixing bowl.

Add milk and clam liquid.

Sift in the flour, baking powder, salt and peppers.

Add clams and parsley flakes. Mix together. Batter should be slightly thicker than pancake batter. Adjust by adding either milk or a little flour.

Heat shortening or oil 2" deep to 375 degrees in fryer.

Using soup spoon, drop mixture into hot shortening and fry until golden brown. (Although the cakes are round, if batter is correct consistency, delicious "spines" will form as the batter falls from the spoon into the hot fat.)

Drain on paper towel. Taste one and add more salt and pepper if desired.

Serve hot with clam chowder.

NOTE: To make as hors d'oeuvres, use coffee spoon to measure batter (makes 60).

Minced Clam Fritters

INGREDIENTS (Makes about 24)

2	Cups	Clams, coarsely chopped, with liquid
1		Egg
4	Tbls.	All purpose flour
1/4	Tsp.	Baking powder
1/4	Tsp.	Salt
1/8	Tsp.	Pepper
		Shortening or salad oil for frying

DIRECTIONS

Drain clams and retain liquid.

In a large mixing bowl, mix together the clams, egg, flour, baking powder, salt and pepper.

Add just enough liquid to make a thick batter.

Heat 1/2" shortening or oil in a 12" frying pan to 375 degrees.

Drop batter by spoonfuls into hot shortening, a few spoonfuls at a time.

Fry 4 to 5 minutes until golden brown on both sides.

Drain well on paper towels.

Garnish with parsley sprigs and lemon wedges.

Serve with tartar sauce or seafood sauce.

Whole Clam Fritters

INGREDIENTS (makes about 24)

2 1/2	Cups	All purpose flour
1 1/2	Tsp.	Salt
1 1/2	Tsp.	Baking powder
1/4	Cup	Butter or margerine
3		Eggs, separated
1	Cup	Beer
2	Cups	Medium size clams, shucked, with liquid
1/2	Cup	Onion, finely diced
1/8	Tsp.	Garlic powder
1/8	Tsp.	Pepper
1	Tbl.	Parsley, chopped
		Shortening or salad oil for frying

DIRECTIONS

Put flour, salt and baking powder in a large bowl.

Melt butter and add to mixture.

Lightly beat egg yolks and mix in well.

While mixing, gradually add the beer.

Place in warm spot and allow to stand for 1 hour.

Add clams with liquid, onion, garlic, pepper and parsely.

Mix into fairly thick batter, adding more flour or beer as required.

Beat egg whites until stiff and fold in.

Heat shortening 1" deep to 375 degrees in 12" frying pan.

Drop batter by tablespoon, each containing a clam, in hot shortening.

Cook for 4 to 5 minutes until golden brown on both sides.

Drain well on paper towel. Taste one and adjust seasonings.

Garnish with parsley sprigs and lemon wedges.

Serve with tartar sauce or seafood sauce.

Quick Whole Clam Fritters

INGREDIENTS (makes about 24)

2	Cups	Medium size clams, shucked, with liquid
1	Cup	Soda cracker crumbs
1	Cup	All purpose flour
1	Tsp.	Salt
1/8	Tsp.	Pepper
1	Cup	Milk
		Shortening or salad oil for frying

DIRECTIONS

Drain clam liquid into small bowl.

Mix dry ingredients together well in separate bowl.

Dip clam into clam liquid and then cover with flour mixture.

Dip clam into liquid and flour mixture twice again.

Dip clam into milk and once again in flour mixture.

Heat 1/2" of shortening or oil in 12" frying pan to 375 degrees.

Drop in clams a few at a time, and fry 4 to 5 minutes until golden brown on both sides.

Drain thoroughly on paper towel. Taste one and adjust seasonings.

Garnish with parsley sprigs and lemon wedges.

Serve with tartar sauce or seafood sauce.

Raw Potato Quahaug Patties

INGREDIENTS (makes 18 patties)

2	Cups	Clams, shucked, with liquid
4		Potatoes, peeled and quartered
2		Onions, quartered
2		Eggs
3	Tbls.	All purpose flour
1	Tsp.	Baking powder
2	Tbls.	Grated Parmesan cheese
1/2	Tsp.	Salt
1/8	Tsp.	Pepper
2	Tbls.	Parsley, chopped
2	Tbls.	Salad oil or hot fat

DIRECTIONS

Coarsely grind clams, potatoes and onions.

Add eggs, flour, cheese, salt, pepper and parsley.

Mix together to form a thick batter, adding either more flour or a little water as required.

Heat salad oil in 12" frying pan to 375 degrees.

Drop 1/3 cup mounds of mixture into pan and flatten into a 4" patty with pancake turner.

Fry patties until golden on both sides.

Remove patties to warm platter and keep warm.

Repeat with remaining potato mixture, adding more oil as required.

Serve with catsup or chili sauce.

Clam Patties

INGREDIENTS (makes 10 patties)

2	Cups	Clams, minced, with liquid
2	Tbls.	Butter
1/4	Cup	Onion, minced
1/2	Cup	Celery, minced
1/2	Cup	Bread crumbs
2		Eggs
1/2	Cup	Cream
1/8	Tsp.	Pepper
1/2	Tsp.	Paprika
1/2	Tsp.	Salt
2	Tbls.	Parsley, chopped
1/2	Tsp.	Dry mustard
1/4	Cup	Bread crumbs
1	Tbl.	Butter

DIRECTIONS

Drain clams and reserve liquid.

Melt butter and saute onion and celery for 3 minutes.

Add bread crumbs, mix and remove from heat.

Beat eggs slightly in a mixing bowl. Add cream and mix.

Add the sauted mixture, clams, pepper, paprika, salt, parsley and mustard.

Add just enough clam liquid to make a thick dough.

Chill for 2 hours.

Form into patties 3" diameter by 1/2" deep.

Dust with bread crumbs.

Melt butter in 12" frying pan.

Brown cakes quickly on both sides.

Lower heat and cook slowly for about 6 minutes longer.

Garnish with parsley and lemon wedges.

Quick Clam Patties

INGREDIENTS (makes 4 to 6 patties)

2	Cups	Clams, with liquid
1		Egg
1	Cup	Cracker crumbs
1/2	Tsp.	Salt
1/4	Tsp.	Pepper
		Shortening or salad oil for frying

DIRECTIONS

Drain clams and reserve liquid.

Beat egg in a mixing bowl.

Add clams, cracker crumbs, salt and pepper.

Add liquid and mix until a thick dough is formed.

Form into patties, 3" in diameter by 1/2" thick.

Heat shortening 1/4" deep to 375 degrees in 12" skillet.

Fry 3 to 5 minutes until golden brown on each side.

Drain on paper towel.

Serve with parsley and lemon wedges.

Fried

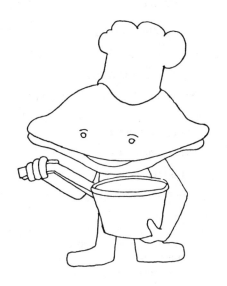

Dip and Roll Fried Clams

INGREDIENTS (serves 3 or 4)

1		Egg
1	Tbl.	Milk
1	Cup	Dry bread crumbs, cracker crumbs, all purpose flour, cornmeal, potato chips or a combination of any two
1	Tsp.	Salt
1/8	Tsp.	Pepper
1/8	Tsp.	Paprika
2	Cups	Soft shell clams, shucked, with liquid*
		Shortening or salad oil for deep frying

DIRECTIONS

Beat eggs in a small bowl and add milk.

In a separate bowl, mix dry ingredients.

Dip clams in egg mixture and roll in dry mixture.

Heat shortening in deep fat fryer to 375 degrees.

Fry clams, several at a time, until they float and are golden brown, about 2 to 3 minutes.**

Drain on paper towel. Salt lightly.

Garnish with lemon wedge and parsley sprig.

Serve plain or with tartar sauce, seafood sauce or butter sauce.***

NOTES: *Discard the black covering over "neck" and along the shell.
    ** As an alternate to shortening, saute the clams in 1/2 cup of butter in frying pan for 3 to 4 minutes on each side.
*** See recipe on page 68.

Dry Mix Fried Clams

INGREDIENTS (serves 1 or 2)

2	Cups	Pancake mix (regular or buttermilk)
1/2	Tsp.	Salt
1/4	Tsp.	Pepper
1	Cup	Soft shell clams, shucked and drained*
		Shortening or salad oil for deep frying

DIRECTIONS

Place the pancake mix, salt and pepper into mixing bowl and mix.

Add a handful of clams and toss lightly with both hands until well coated. Shake off excess in wire basket.

Heat shortening to 375 degrees in deep fryer.

Fry clams until they float and are golden brown, about 2 to 3 minutes.

Drain on paper towels and salt lightly.

Garnish with lemon wedges and parsley sprigs.

Serve with tartar sauce, seafood sauce or melted butter.

NOTE: *Discard the black covering over the "neck" and along the shell.

Butter Sauce for Fried Clams

INGREDIENTS (serves 2 to 4)

1/4	Pound	Butter
2	Tbls.	Parsley
1/8	Tsp.	Tabasco sauce

DIRECTIONS

Melt the butter.

Add the parsley and Tabasco sauce.

Pour over clams or serve in small dishes for dipping clams.

Quick Batter Fried Clams

INGREDIENTS (serves 3 or 4)

2	Cups	Soft shell clams, shucked, with liquid*
2		Eggs
1	Cup	Milk
2	Cups	All purpose flour, sifted
4	Tsp.	Baking powder
1/2	Tsp.	Salt
1/2	Tsp.	Pepper
1/2	Tsp.	Paprika
1	Tbl.	Grated onion
		Shortening or salad oil for frying

DIRECTIONS

Drain clams and save liquid.

Beat the eggs in a mixing bowl.

Add the milk and 1/2 cup of clam liquid.

Mix in the flour, baking powder, salt, pepper, paprika and onion.

Heat the shortening in a deep fryer to 375 degrees.

Dip each clam into the batter and then drop into fryer.

Fry until they float and are golden brown, about 3 minutes.

Drain on paper towel and salt lightly.

Garnish with lemon slices and parsley sprigs.

Serve with tartar sauce or seafood sauce.

NOTE: *Discard the black covering over the "neck" and along the shell.

Batter Fried Clams

INGREDIENTS (serves 1 or 2)

2		Eggs
1/2	Cup	Milk
1	Tsp.	Olive oil
1	Tbl.	Lemon juice
1	Cup	All purpose flour
1	Cup	Soft shell clams, shucked, drained of liquid*
1	Cup	Shortening or salad oil for deep frying

DIRECTIONS

Beat the egg yolks and then add milk, oil, lemon juice and flour.

Add the clams and stir.

Refrigerate for 2 hours.

Heat shortening in deep fryer to 375 degrees.

Drop clams, one at a time, into hot fat.

Fry until they float and are golden brown, about 3 minutes.

Drain on paper towel and salt lightly.

Garnish with lemon wedge and parsley flakes.

Serve with tartar sauce or seafood sauce.

NOTE: *Discard the black covering over the "neck" and along the shell.

Boils and Bakes

Steamed Clams

INGREDIENTS (serves 6)

6	Quarts	Soft shell steamer clams
1	Cup	Water
		Butter, melted
		Salt
		Pepper

DIRECTIONS

Wash clams thoroughly.

Place clams in large kettle or top section of clam steamer.

Add water.

Cover tightly and steam for 5 to 10 minutes, until clam shells open. (Overcooking will toughen clams.)

Drain clams and reserve liquid. Strain liquid.

Serve clams hot in shells together with a cup of the hot liquid and a container of melted butter.

TO EAT THE CLAMS

Remove the clam from shell, discarding the inedible black neck sheath from neck and along shell seam.

Dip the clam in broth to wash away any remaining sand.

Dip in melted butter and eat.

TO DRINK THE BROTH

Add a little butter to the broth, season with salt and pepper.

The broth is delicious, but don't drain the entire cup, there may be some sand on the bottom.

VARIATION

Use littleneck or cherrystone (hard shell) clams. Follow directions above for cooking. When eating, the entire clam is edible (no black neck sheath).

Basque Style Steamed Clams
(Almejas Guisadas)

INGREDIENTS (serves 4 to 6)

4	Quarts	Cherrystone clams
4	Cloves	Garlic, minced
1		Onion, about 1" in diameter, minced
1	Tbl.	Parsley, minced
1	Tbl.	Olive oil
1/2	Cup	Dry white wine
1/2	Cup	Water (or additional clam liquid)
1/4	Tsp.	Black pepper, freshly ground

DIRECTIONS

Wash clams thoroughly and place in large kettle.

Add remaining ingredients.

Cover and cook over medium heat for 20 minutes.

Serve hot in individual bowls, accompanied by thick slices of French bread and a green salad.

Clam Boil

INGREDIENTS (serves 6)

3	Quarts	Soft shell steamer clams
6		Onions, 1 1/2", whole, peeled
6		Potatoes, 2", in jacket, scrubbed
4		Carrots, scrubbed, tips removed and cut into 2" lengths
6	Links	Pork sausage, wrapped in wax paper
9	Ears	Corn on the cob, in the husks, previously dipped in ocean or salted water
6		Lobsters, 1 pound each, live

DIRECTIONS

Layer all the ingredients in a large kettle or steamer in the order given.

Add 1 cup of water and cover tightly.

Place on stove or fire. Begin timing as soon as steam is seen. Adjust heat so that just a tiny bit of steam escapes continuously. Cook slowly for exactly 1 hour.

Serve hot.

TO EAT

This meal is best eaten in three courses. First eat the clams (see directions with recipes for steamed clams). Then eat all the vegetables and sausage. The lobster, naturally, is the dessert!

Traditional New England Clambake

TIMETABLE:

A clambake is a grand affair that takes the whole day, with a swim after the fire is lit and again after the bake has been laid. Allow time to clean up before the sun goes down. Then enjoy a bonfire.

12:00 noon	Dig pit and line with stones.
1:00 p.m.	Light the fire.
3:00 p.m.	Prepare individual bakes.
3:45 p.m.	Lay the bake.
5:00 p.m.	Serve clams and beer.
5:30 p.m.	Serve the individual bakes.
6:30 p.m.	Serve watermelon and coffee.

EQUIPMENT, ETC.

To dig a pit: a shovel.

To line the pit: stones, about the size of cabbages, 4" to 8" in diameter. Use only *dry* stones, as wet stones can explode. Do not use stones which have been used before, as they will not properly retain heat. Also, do not use soft stones that crumble or are extremely porous (i.e., flat sand stone).

To heat the stones: lots of dry wood.

To remove the embers and ashes: a rake or board

To separate stones from bake: a 5' square piece of chicken wire.

To provide the water for steam: rockweed (the long, lacy, dark green type of seaweed that has many egg-shaped pods that pop when pressed). Gather about 4 bushels of rockweed. It will be found attached to rocks in shallow water, at low tide. Wash it and keep it soaking in salt water until time to use.

To hold fish and sausage: small paper sandwich bags.

To make up individual bakes: one piece of 18" square cheesecloth *per person*, plus a few extra pieces to hold the clams.

To retain the steam: an 8' square piece of clean canvas, without any holes.

INGREDIENTS (per person)

1		Whole lobster, 1 to 1 1/2 pounds, live (If you're having your bake along the Chesapeake Bay, substitute 3 or 4 hard shell crabs for the lobster)
1	Ear	Corn on the cob, with outer layer of husks and silk removed, dipped in salt water or sea water
1	Quarter	Chicken (optional), browned on grill but not cooked
1		Whole baking potato, sweet potato or yam, 2", in skin, scrubbed
1	Piece	Fish (preferably bluefish), 2" square, in small paper bag
1		Whole onion, 1 1/2", peeled and washed
1	Link	Sausage, in small paper bag
1	Quart	Soft shell steamer clams, well scrubbed
		Butter, melted
		Salt
		Pepper

This may seem like a lot of food, but once each person gets a whiff of the steam coming from the bake, they will become ravenously hungry for the anticipated feast.

DIRECTIONS

Dig a pit in the sand, well above the high water mark. Make it about 1' deep and 3' in diameter, shaped like a large bowl. This will be large enough to accomodate a bake for up to 20 people.

Place a layer of stones around the bottom and sides of the pit, until the pit is completely lined. Fill in gaps with smaller stones. The top will now be almost level with the ground.

Build a big wood fire over the entire pit and burn it until it dies down and the stones are white hot. This will take from 2 to 3 hours.

Toward the end of the time that the fire is burning down, prepare an individual bake for each guest.

Kill the lobster by inserting a sharp knife through the back into the joint where the tail and body shell come together, to cut spinal cord.

Spread out a piece of cheesecloth and place the lobster in the center.

Add the corn, chicken, potato, fish, onion and sausage.

Gather up the corners and tie securely to provide an individual package for each guest.

Divide the clams and prepare several cheesecloths containing only clams. They will go on top of the bake and be served first.

Now, working quickly so the stones will not cool, lay the bake:

Make certain the rocks are white hot. Uncover one of the rocks and drop a teaspoon of water on it. If it evaporates almost immediately, the stones are ready.

Scrape the embers and ashes out of the pit.

Cover the stones with a 4" to 6" layer of wet rockweed. Make certain the rockweed covers all the stones.

Place the chicken wire over the rockweed.

Pile the individual bakes on the wire.

Place the bags of clams on top.

Cover with 4" to 6" of additional wet rockweed. (This step is optional. Many say it is unnecessary and that the canvas alone is better.)

Place one potato on top.

Wet the canvas in salt water and cover the bake.

Weigh down the edges of the canvas with stones and sand to prevent the escape of *any* steam.

After 1/2 hour, sprinkle a bucket of salt water over the top of the canvas, to add more water for steam.

After 1 hour from the time the bake started, pull up a corner of the canvas and test the potato. If tender, the bake is ready.

Remove the canvas, the top layer of rockweed and the cheesecloths containing the clams.

Replace the canvas over the rest of the bake.

Serve the clams with a container of melted butter and a cold beer.

To prepare the clams for eating, remove and discard the black sheath from the neck and along the rim of the shell. Then, dip the clam in butter and enjoy!

After the clams are finished, again remove the canvas and distribute the individual bakes with another container of melted butter to each guest. Pass salt and pepper.

Serve chunks of watermelon and hot coffee for dessert.

Clams Steamed in Beer

INGREDIENTS (serves 4)

3	Quarts	Soft shell steamer clams, cleaned
3/4	Cup	Beer
1	Small	Onion, chopped
1/4	Tsp.	Dried oregano
1/2	Tsp.	Black pepper, freshly ground
1	Stick	Butter
1	Tsp.	Fresh lemon juice

DIRECTIONS

Place the steamers in a large pot. Add the beer, onion, oregano and pepper. Cover and place over high heat. Bring to a boil and cook, shaking the pan frequently, until clams open, about 10 minutes.

Transfer clams to a serving dish, using a slotted spoon. Discard any that do not open. Strain broth into individual cups.

Melt butter in a small saucepan and blend in the lemon juice. Pour into four individual cups. Serve clams piping hot, with dishes of clam broth and butter.

Sauces

Clam Sauce for Pasta

INGREDIENTS (serves 4)

4	Tbls.	Olive oil
2	Cloves	Garlic, minced
2	Cups	Clams, minced, with liquid
1/2	Tsp.	Salt
1/8	Tsp.	Black pepper, ground
1/4	Cup	Parsley, finely chopped

DIRECTIONS

Place all ingredients in saucepan and heat to a simmer.

Toss hot cooked spaghetti with the clam sauce.

Serve with additional chopped parsley.

White Clam Sauce

INGREDIENTS (serves 4 to 6)

1	Clove	Garlic, finely diced
3	Tbls.	Olive oil
1	Tbl.	Parsley, chopped fine
3		Whole anchovies, diced, or 2 teaspoons anchovy paste
2	Cups	Clams, chopped, with liquid
1/4	Tsp.	Black pepper, ground
1	Dash	Cayenne pepper

DIRECTIONS

Saute garlic lightly in oil.

Add parsley and stir once or twice.

Add anchovies, clams and seasonings.

Bring to a boil and simmer for 2 minutes.

Adjust seasonings.

Serve over hot cooked and drained spaghetti.

Quick Red Clam Sauce

INGREDIENTS (serves 4)

2	Tbls.	Butter
1	Tbl.	Olive oil
2	Cloves	Garlic, minced
2	Cups	Clams, minced, with liquid
1	Cup	Tomato sauce
1/2	Cup	Dry white wine
1/2	Tsp.	Salt
1/8	Tsp.	Black pepper, ground
1	Tbl.	Parsley, chopped
1	Tsp.	Basil

DIRECTIONS

Heat butter and olive oil in saucepan.

Lightly saute garlic.

Add clams, tomato sauce, wine, salt, pepper, parsley and basil.

Stir well and simmer uncovered for about 10 minutes.

Adjust seasonings.

Serve over hot cooked and drained spaghetti with grated Parmesan cheese.

Mexican Style Clam Sauce

INGREDIENTS (serves 4)

1	Can	Italian plum tomatos (8 ounces)
2	Cups	Clams, minced
2	Tsp.	Chili powder
1	Tsp.	Paprika
3	Drops	Tabasco sauce
2	Tbls.	Olive oil
1		Onion, about 3" in diameter, finely chopped
1	Cup	Black olives, pitted and thinly sliced
		Salt
		Black pepper, freshly ground

DIRECTIONS

Thoroughly drain the juice from the tomatos and clams into a small saucepan. Add the chili powder, paprika and Tabasco sauce.

Bring liquid to a simmer over medium heat. Cook, uncovered, stirring occasionally, until liquid is reduced by half.

While liquid is reducing, heat olive oil in heavy skillet. Add onions and olives. Saute until onions are golden.

Stir in tomatos and clams. Simmer for 3 minutes.

Add reduced sauce, stir and season to taste with salt and pepper.

Serve sauce hot over Mexican Rice (see following recipe.)

Mexican Rice

INGREDIENTS (serves 4)

5	Tsp.	Olive oil
1	Cup	White rice (non-instant)
1		Onion, about 1" in diameter, finely chopped
1	Clove	Garlic, finely diced
1		Carrot, about 1" in diameter, thinly sliced
1	Can	Tiny peas (8 ounces)
1	Can	Tomato sauce (8 ounces)
1	Can	Undiluted condensed chicken broth (13 3/4 ounces)
1	Tbl.	Coriander, ground
2	Tbls.	Parsley, chopped

DIRECTIONS

Heat olive oil in heavy skillet.

When hot, add rice and stir until opaque and golden.

Add onion, garlic and carrot. Saute lightly.

Stir in juice from peas, tomato sauce and chicken broth.

Bring to a boil, stir once, cover and reduce heat to very low.

Cook for 30 minutes, or until all liquid is absorbed.

Stir in peas, cover and keep warm until ready to serve.

Garnish with coriander and parsley flakes before serving.

Whole Clam Sauce

INGREDIENTS (makes 2 quarts of sauce)

1 1/2	Tbls.	Olive oil
3	Cloves	Garlic, finely chopped
1	Cup	Onion, finely chopped
1	Can	Tomato puree (29 ounces)
2	Cans	Tomato paste (6 ounces)
1/4	Tsp.	Salt
1/4	Tsp.	Black pepper
1 1/2	Tbls.	Worcestershire sauce
2	Tsp.	Oregano
4	Tsp.	Parsley
1 1/2	Cups	Dry white wine (Chablis)
6	Dozen	Cherrystone or littleneck clams, well scrubbed

DIRECTIONS

Pour oil into 4 or 5 quart dutch oven. Saute garlic and onion at medium/low heat until soft. Don't brown.

Add puree, paste, salt, pepper, Worcestershire sauce, oregano, parsley and wine.

Cover and simmer for 30 minutes, stirring periodically.*

Add clams and simmer about 5 minutes, until clams open.

SERVING SUGGESTIONS

Place cooked clams in shells around the edge of a platter of spaghetti and spoon sauce liberally over top.

Spoon 12 clams per person into soup tureen, and add 3 or 4 large spoonfuls of sauce. Serve as a soup with French bread.

Add a can or two of chopped clams to leftover sauce and freeze for later, then serve as above with spaghetti.

NOTE: *Sauce is now ready, either for finishing and serving or to save for use at a later time.

Clam Stroganoff

INGREDIENTS (serves 4)

5	Tbls.	Butter
2		Onions, 2", sliced
1/2	Pound	Mushrooms, wiped and sliced
1/2	Tsp.	Salt
1/4	Tsp.	Black pepper
2	Tbls.	Flour
1	Cup	Clam liquid
1	Cup	Clams, minced and drained
1	Cup	Sour cream
1	Tbl.	Parsley, chopped
		Cooked egg noodles, hot

DIRECTIONS

Melt butter in large skillet or dutch oven.

Add onions and saute until transparent.

Add mushrooms, salt and pepper. Saute until mushrooms are tender.

Sprinkle flour over mixture and gradually add the clam liquid, stirring constantly, until a sauce has been made.

Add the clams and simmer for 3 minutes.

Place the sour cream in a small bowl. Gradually add 1 cup of the hot clam mixture, 1/3 of a cup at a time, while stirring continually.

Pour this sour cream mixture back into the skillet. Add about half the parsley and heat to just below boiling.

Serve over hot buttered egg noodles, garnished with the remaining parsley.

Linguine with Clam Sauce

INGREDIENTS (serves 2)

1/4	Cup	Butter (1/2 stick)
1	Medium	Onion, diced (about 1 cup)
3	Cloves	Garlic, minced
1	Tsp.	Flour
1	Can	Minced clams (6-1/2 ounce)
1/2	Cup	Milk
2	Tsps.	Parsley flakes
		Salt
		Black pepper, freshly ground
4	Ounces	Linguine, cooked and drained

DIRECTIONS

Melt the butter in a medium saucepan over medium heat. Add onion and garlic, and saute until golden. Blend in the flour.

Reduce heat and add the clams and milk. Cover and simmer for 10 minutes. Add parsley and season to taste with salt and pepper.

Serve over the linguine.

With Eggs

Clam Soufflé

INGREDIENTS (serves 6)

3	Tbls.	Butter
2	Cups	Clams, chopped, with liquid
3	Tbls.	Flour
1/2	Tsp.	Salt
1/8	Tsp.	Pepper
1/8	Tsp.	Nutmeg
3		Eggs, separated

DIRECTIONS

Melt butter in saucepan.

Drain clams, reserving liquid.

Saute clams in butter for 3 minutes. Remove clams.

Add flour and seasonings to butter and stir over low heat.

Add enough water to clam liquid to make 1 cup.

Gradually add clam liquid to butter/flour mixture, stirring constantly, until a smooth sauce forms.

Stir a little of this sauce into beaten egg yolks. Add to remaining sauce, stirring constantly.

Add cooked clams.

Beat egg whites until stiff, but still moist.

Fold in egg whites. Do not overmix.

Pour into greased 1 quart casserole or souffle dish.

Bake at 350 degrees for 45 minutes, until the souffle is puffed up and brown.

Serve immediately, with or without sauce.

Clam and Corn Soufflé

INGREDIENTS (serves 4)

1	Cup	Clams, minced, with liquid
1	Can	Whole kernel corn (12 ounces)
5		Egg yolks
1/2	Tsp.	Salt
1	Dash	Tabasco sauce
6		Egg whites, stiffly beaten

DIRECTIONS

Blend together the clams, corn, egg yolks, salt and Tabasco.

Fold in the egg whites and pour mixture into a buttered 1 1/2 quart souffle dish.

Bake in preheated 375 degree oven for 30 minutes or until top is puffed up and delicately browned.

Clam Spinach Timbale

INGREDIENTS (serves 6)

2	Packages	Spinach (10 ounces), frozen, chopped
2	Cups	Clams, with liquid
5	Tbls.	Butter
1/2	Cup	Onion, chopped
3	Tbls.	Flour
1	Cup	Light cream
4		Eggs, beaten
1/2	Tsp.	Salt
1/2	Tsp.	Mace
1/4	Tsp.	Pepper
1 1/2	Cups	Gruyere cheese, grated
3	Cups	Egg noodles, cooked and buttered
1		Lime, sliced

DIRECTIONS

Prepare spinach according to package directions. Drain very well.

Chop clams and drain, reserving 1/2 cup liquid.

Melt butter in saucepan.

Saute onions until golden.

Add clams and saute 3 minutes.

Add flour and stir until blended.

Gradually add cream and clam liquid, stirring constantly, until a sauce is made.

Simmer for 1 minute. Remove from heat and allow to cool slightly.

In a bowl, blend together eggs, clams, salt, mace, pepper, cheese and spinach.

Add sauce and fold together.

Pour into a well-greased 5 cup ring mold.

Set mold in large baking pan in preheated oven. Add 1" of water.

Bake at 325 degrees for 40 minutes.

Allow to cool slightly and invert onto platter.

Fill center with hot buttered egg noodles. Garnish with lime.

Clam Omelette-Soufflé

INGREDIENTS (serves 2 or 3)

1	Cup	Clams, chopped, with liquid
6		Eggs, separated
1	Tbl.	Butter
1/2	Tsp.	Salt
1/8	Tsp.	Pepper, freshly ground

DIRECTIONS

Drain clams, reserving liquid.

Beat egg yolks until light. Add 6 tablespoons of clam liquid.

Beat egg whites until stiff, but still moist.

Melt butter in skillet. Tip skillet so that butter touches sides as well as bottom.

Saute clams for 3 minutes over low flame.

Remove clams and add to egg yolk mixture.

Fold egg whites into mixture. Do not overmix.

Pour mixture into skillet and cook slowly, until bubbles show on top.

Place in preheated 325 degree oven for 5 minutes, or until omelette is dry on top.

Remove from skillet, fold over and serve immediately.

Clam Mushroom Soufflé

INGREDIENTS (serves 4)

4	Tbls.	Butter
1/2	Cup	Mushrooms, sliced
1	Cup	Clams, with liquid
2		Eggs, beaten
1	Can	Condensed cream of mushroom soup (10 1/2 ounces)
1	Cup	Milk
30		Ritz crackers, crushed
1/8	Tsp.	Pepper

DIRECTIONS

Chop clams and drain. Reserve liquid.

Melt butter in frying pan.

Saute mushrooms over medium heat until edges are golden.

Add drained clams, lower heat and saute for 3 minutes.

Put the clam liquid and all remaining ingredients in bowl.

Add clams, mushrooms and butter. Mix together.

Pour into greased 1 1/2 quart casserole.

Place in preheated oven and bake at 350 degrees for 30 minutes.

Shrimp and Clam Soufflé

INGREDIENTS (serves 6)

1	Cup	Clams, minced, with liquid
1/2	Pound	Raw shrimp, peeled and deveined
1	Tsp.	Dill weed (or 1 tablespoon fresh dill)
1	Tsp.	Salt
1/2	Tsp.	Black pepper, freshly ground
5		Egg yolks
6		Egg whites

DIRECTIONS

Put all ingredients except egg whites in an electric blender and blend for 30 seconds.

Beat the egg whites until stiff, but not dry.

Remove mixture from blender and fold in 1/3 of egg whites rather thoroughly.

Fold in remaining egg whites very lightly.

Pour mixture into 6 buttered souffle dishes, no more than 2/3 full.

Place individual dishes in a pan of hot water in a preheated 375 degree oven. Bake for 15 to 17 minutes.

Serve with hollandaise sauce.

VARIATION (1 large souffle)

Pour mixture into 1 large buttered souffle dish, no more than 2/3 full.

Place souffle dish in a pan of hot water.

Place in a preheated 375 degree oven and bake for 30 minutes.

Hollandaise Sauce

INGREDIENTS (makes 1 1/2 cups)

4		Egg yolks
2	Tbls.	Lemon juice
1/2	Tsp.	Salt
1/2	Tsp.	Dry mustard
3	Drops	Tabasco sauce
1	Cup	Butter, melted and heated almost to the boiling point

DIRECTIONS

Place the egg yolks, juice and seasonings in blender and blend for 1 second. (Do not overblend.)

Remove cover and pour in bubbling hot butter in a thin steady stream, as the mixture blends.

Blend until smooth and creamy, but do not overblend.

Steamed Eggs With Clams

INGREDIENTS (serves 2)

2		Eggs
1	Tsp.	Salt
2	Tsp.	Dry sherry wine
1/2	Tsp.	Sugar
2	Tsp.	Water
1/2	Tsp.	Monosodium glutamate
12		Littleneck or cherrystone clams, in shells, well scrubbed
		Sesame oil, few drops
		Soy sauce, few drops

DIRECTIONS

Beat eggs. Add salt, wine, sugar, water, MSG and clams.

Place in a steamer or the top of a double boiler.

Steam mixture for 15 minutes over boiling water.

Before serving, sprinkle with sesame oil and soy sauce.

One Dish Meals, Casseroles, Hash and Pies

Clams With Ginger and Coconut

INGREDIENTS (serves 4 to 6)

1		Large onion, finely chopped
1/4	Cup	Oil
1	Clove	Garlic, finely minced
1	Piece	Ginger root, 1", finely minced
2		Fresh green hot chili peppers, seeded and cut into thin rings
2	Tsp.	Ground cumin
1/2	Tsp.	Tumeric
1/2	Tsp.	Salt
2	Cups	Grated coconut, loosely packed
24		Littleneck or cherrystone clams, scrubbed

DIRECTIONS

In a heavy skillet, saute onion until soft.

Add garlic, ginger, peppers, cumin, tumeric, salt and 1/3 cup of water. Saute for 2 minutes.

Add coconut and 1 additional cup water. Saute mixture for 2 more minutes.

Add clams. Cover tightly and steam for 5 minutes, or just until clam shells open.

Serve immediately.

Clam Puff

INGREDIENTS (serves 4)

6	Slices	White bread, cubed
1 1/2	Cups	American cheese, grated
2	Cups	Clams, coarsely cut, with liquid
1	Tbl.	Onion, grated
1/4	Tsp.	Salt
1/8	Tsp.	Pepper
2		Eggs, slightly beaten
1	Cup	Milk
1/8	Tsp.	Worcestershire sauce
2	Drops	Tabasco sauce
1	Tsp.	Minced parsley

DIRECTIONS

Place half the bread cubes in a greased 2 quart casserole.

Place a layer of cheese on top of the bread, then all of the clams, the onion and the rest of the cheese. Cover with the remaining bread cubes and sprinkle with salt and pepper.

Mix together the eggs, milk, Worcestershire sauce, Tabasco sauce and parsley. Pour it over the mixture in the casserole.

Bake in a preheated 325 degree oven for 1 hour.

Scalloped Clams

INGREDIENTS (serves 4 to 6)

3	Cups	Clams, finely chopped, with liquid
1	Cup	Cracker crumbs
1	Tbl.	Butter
1	Tbl.	Flour
1	Cup	Milk
1/2	Tsp.	Poultry seasoning
1/2	Tsp.	Salt
1/2	Cup	Buttered crumbs
1/8	Tsp.	Paprika

DIRECTIONS

Arrange the clams and cracker crumbs in layers in a buttered baking dish.

Melt the butter in a skillet, stir in flour and gradually add the milk, stirring constantly.

Add the poultry seasoning and salt to this sauce and pour over the clams.

Top with buttered crumbs and sprinkle with paprika.

Bake in a preheated 375 degree oven for 1/2 hour or until nicely browned.

Serve hot.

Creamed Clams

INGREDIENTS (serves 4)

50		Soft shell steamer clams
3		Egg yolks
1	Pint	Heavy cream
1/2	Cup	Water
1	Tbl.	Sherry, dry
1/4	Tsp.	Salt
1/8	Tsp.	Black pepper, freshly ground
2	Tbls.	Parmesan cheese, grated

DIRECTIONS

Steam the clams. Remove from shells, trim and chop slightly. Place clams in buttered casserole.

Beat egg yolks, cream and water with rotary egg beater. Season with sherry, salt and pepper.

Pour sauce over clams in casserole. Sprinkle with cheese.

Bake in preheated 325 degree oven for 20 minutes.

Serve hot in casserole.

NOTE: This recipe makes excellent use of clams left over from a clam bake, clam boil or a meal of steamed clams.

Minced Clams

INGREDIENTS (serves 4)

4	Tbls.	Butter
4	Quarts	Cherrystone clams, shucked and coarsely chopped, with liquid
1	Tbl.	Parsley, finely chopped
1	Tbl.	Celery leaves, finely chopped
1	Tbl.	Lemon juice
1/4	Tsp.	Salt
1/8	Tsp.	Black pepper, freshly ground
1/3	Cup	Dry white wine

DIRECTIONS

Melt butter in saucepan.

Add clams and liquid. Simmer gently for about 2 minutes.

Add parsley, celery, lemon juice, salt, pepper and wine. Heat thoroughly but do not allow to boil.

Serve in individual casseroles or ramekins with hot buttered toast fingers.

Clam Stuffed Eggplant

INGREDIENTS (serves 4)

1		Large eggplant
1/4	Cup	Onion, minced
1/4	Cup	Butter
1	Cup	Clams, minced, with liquid
2	Tbls.	Parsley, minced
1/4	Tsp.	Basil
1	Cup	Soft French bread crumbs
		Salt
		Pepper
1/2	Cup	Soft French bread crumbs
2	Tbls.	Butter, melted

DIRECTIONS

Cut top from eggplant and scoop out pulp, taking care to leave shell intact.

Chop pulp and steam until tender.

Melt butter in skillet and saute onion until transparent.

Add clams, parsley, basil, the pulp, 1 cup of crumbs, salt and pepper to taste.

Fill shell with the mixture.

Mix 1/2 cup crumbs with 2 tablespoons melted butter and sprinkle onto filling.

Bake in a preheated 350 degree oven about 30 minutes.

Eggplant With Clam Stuffing

INGREDIENTS (serves 4 to 6)

4	Tbls.	Cooking oil
1		Large eggplant, cut in half lengthwise, with flesh scored in a crisscross pattern with a few shallow slashes
2	Tbls.	Butter
1		Onion, about 1 1/2" in diameter, finely chopped
1	Cup	Soft bread crumbs
1	Cup	Clams, minced, with liquid reserved
1		Egg, beaten
2	Tbls.	Parsley, minced
1/2	Tsp.	Thyme
1/4	Tsp.	Salt
1/8	Tsp.	Black pepper, freshly ground
		Bread crumbs
		Grated Parmesan cheese

DIRECTIONS

Heat oil in a large skillet. Add the eggplant halves, cut side down. Cover skillet and cook over low heat for 20 minutes.

Remove eggplant and scoop out flesh, leaving a 1/4" layer on the skins to keep them whole.

Melt butter in a clean skillet. Add onion and saute until transparent.

Chop the eggplant flesh and add to skillet along with the bread crumbs, clams, reserved liquid, egg, parsley, thyme, salt and pepper.

Blend the mixture well and stuff the eggplant shells with it.

Sprinkle tops with bread crumbs and cheese.

Bake in a preheated 375 degree oven for 30 minutes.

Rice With Clams

INGREDIENTS (serves 4 to 6)

2	Cups	Water
1/2	Cup	Celery, chopped
3	Tbls.	Onion, chopped
1	Tsp.	Parsley (or 2 sprigs, fresh)
1		Bay leaf
1/2	Tsp.	Marjoram
36		Littleneck or cherrystone clams, well scrubbed
1 1/2	Cups	Rice, uncooked
3/4	Cup	Tomatoes, peeled and chopped
4	Tbls.	Butter
2	Tbls.	Parsley, minced

DIRECTIONS

Bring water, celery, onion, parsley, bay leaf and marjoram to a boil in a large saucepan. Cover and cook over low heat for 10 minutes.

Pour through a sieve and discard celery, onion, parsley and bay leaf.

Add clams. Cover and steam until the clam shells open. Remove clams and discard shells.

Add rice and tomatoes to hot stock. Cover and cook over low heat for about 20 minutes, until rice is tender.

Add the clams and butter. Cook for 2 minutes.

Correct seasonings and transfer to serving dish. Sprinkle with parsley and serve.

Clams and Spaghetti Casserole

INGREDIENTS (serves 6)

3	Tbls.	Butter
1		Onion, about 2" in diameter, finely diced
1	Clove	Garlic, finely diced
1	Cup	Fresh mushrooms, cleaned and sliced
2	Cups	Clams, chopped, with liquid
3	Cans	Tomato sauce (8 ounces)
1	Tsp.	Oregano
1/2	Tsp.	Salt
1/4	Tsp.	Black pepper, freshly ground
1	Pound	Thin spaghetti, broken into 1 1/2" pieces, cooked
1	Cup	Parmesan cheese, grated
1/2	Cup	Bread crumbs

DIRECTIONS

Melt 2 tablespoons of the butter in a skillet. Add the onion and saute gently for 1 minute. Add the garlic and mushroom slices and saute until mushrooms are soft.

Add clams, clam liquid, tomato sauce, oregano, salt and pepper.

In a large casserole, arrange layers of spaghetti, clam sauce, with a little cheese on top of each layer.

Top with remaining cheese and bread crumbs. Dot with remaining tablespoon of butter.

Bake in a preheated 375 degree oven for 30 minutes, or until browned and bubbly.

Quahaug Pie

INGREDIENTS (serves 6 to 8)

8	Cups	Quahaugs, minced, with liquid
2	Cups	Onions, peeled and diced
3	Cups	Potatoes, peeled and diced
1/4	Tsp.	Black pepper
5	Tbls.	Butter
5	Tbls.	Flour
1	Cup	Milk
1 1/2	Cups	Flour
1/2	Cup	Shortening

DIRECTIONS

Drain the quahaugs and reserve liquid.

Put onions and potatoes in a saucepan. Cook in as little quahaug liquid as possible.

Melt butter in a skillet. Add 5 tablespoons of flour and make a paste. Gradually add 1 cup of clam liquid and 1 cup of milk to make a smooth sauce.

In a round baking dish, combine 2/3 of the quahaugs, onions, potatoes and the sauce.

For the crust, blend together 1 1/2 cups of the flour and the shortening. Mix in the remaining quahaugs. They will furnish all the moisture required.

Roll out the crust, rather thick, and place over the baking dish. Attach crust firmly to the edge.

Bake in a preheated 425 degree oven until lightly browned.

Serve hot.

NOTE: Quahaug is the New Englander's name for a large (3"+) hard shell clam.

Deep Dish Quahaug Pie

INGREDIENTS (serves 4)

2	Cups	Quahaugs, chopped, with liquid
1/3	Cup	Salt pork, diced
1	Cup	Onion, chopped
2/3	Cup	Celery tops, chopped
1/3	Cup	Green pepper, chopped
1	Clove	Garlic, minced
1	Cup	Potatoes, diced
1	Cup	Water
1 1/2	Cups	Tomatos, cooked or canned, diced, with liquid
1/8	Cup	Catsup
1/4	Cup	Flour, mixed with 1/2 cup water
1/2	Tsp.	Thyme
1	Tsp.	Parsley, minced
1	Dash	Cayenne pepper, ground
	Dash	Salt
	Dash	Black pepper, ground
2	Cups	Biscuit dough

DIRECTIONS

Drain quahaugs and reserve liquid.

Fry salt pork until light brown.

Add onions, celery, peppers and garlic. Saute until onions are transparent.

Add potatoes, water and clam liquid. Simmer until potatoes are soft.

Add quahaugs, tomatos and catsup. Bring back to simmer.

Add flour and water. Stir until sauce thickens.

Add thyme, parsley, and cayenne pepper and season to taste with salt and pepper.

Pour into 2 quart casserole and cover with biscuit dough.

Bake at 400 degrees until it bubbles; then reduce to 350 degrees for an additional 30 minutes.

Mashed Potato Clam Pie

INGREDIENTS (serves 6)

1/4	Cup	Butter
1	Cup	Onions, chopped
3/4	Cup	Celery, chopped
2	Cups	Clams, minced (reserve liquid)
1/4	Cup	Flour
1/2	Cup	Carrots, diced and cooked
1/4	Tsp.	Salt
1/8	Tsp.	Pepper
1 1/2	Cups	Mashed potatoes, seasoned with milk, butter, salt, pepper and finely chopped chives

DIRECTIONS

Melt butter in frying pan.

Add onions and celery, cook until onions are transparent.

Add clams.

Add clam liquid and enough water to make 2 cups.

Add flour and stir until thickened.

Add carrots.

Season with salt and pepper.

Place mixture in a buttered 1 1/2 quart casserole.

Cover with potatoes.

Bake at 425 degrees until brown, about 20 to 25 minutes.

Old-Fashioned Clam Pie

INGREDIENTS (serves 4)

1/3	Cup	Salt pork, diced
1/2	Cup	Onion, chopped
2	Cups	Clams, chopped, with liquid
1/4	Tsp.	Salt
1/8	Tsp.	Pepper
1	Tbl.	Flour (or enough to thicken mixture)
		Pastry, for 2-crust, 9" pie
2	Tbls.	Milk

DIRECTIONS

Fry salt pork until light brown.

Add onion and fry until transparent.

Add clams and liquid, and cook gently 5 minutes.

Add flour to thicken.

Season with salt and pepper to taste.

Line 9" pie plate with pastry.

Wet outside top 1" of pastry with water.

Pour filling into pastry.

Cover with pastry.

Turn edges under and flute.

Brush with beaten egg or milk for a shiny crust.

Cut slits in top to allow steam to escape.

Bake at 400 degrees for 15 minutes.

Lower to 325 degrees and bake for 25 minutes longer.

Serve very hot.

Deep Dish Clam Pie

INGREDIENTS (4 to 6 servings)

4	Cups	Clams, coarsely chopped, with liquid
1/4	Pound	Butter
4		Potatoes, 3", peeled and thinly sliced
4		Onions, 2", peeled and thinly sliced
1	Tbl.	Flour
1	Tsp.	Salt
1	Tsp.	Pepper
1	Can	Evaporated milk
		Pastry to cover

DIRECTIONS

Drain clams and reserve liquid.

Butter the inside of a 2 quart casserole dish.

Place a layer of potatoes in bottom.

Add a layer of onions.

Add a layer of clams.

Sprinkle with flour.

Season lightly with salt and pepper.

Add balance of potatoes, onions, flour, salt and pepper in layers until dish is nearly full.

Pour in one cup of clam liquid.

Pour in just enough milk to come to top of ingredients.

Cover with pastry crust. Flute edges of crust to decorate. Wash with egg or milk for shiny crust.

Cut slits in top to allow steam to escape.

Bake in preheated 350 degree oven until top is nicely browned and potatoes are done, about 40 minutes

Serve hot from oven.

Sour Cream Clam Pie

INGREDIENTS (serves 6)

1/3	Cup	Bacon, chopped
3		Onions, 2", peeled and chopped
2	Cups	Small whole clams
1/2	Tsp.	Salt
1/8	Tsp.	Pepper
1/8	Cup	Flour
2		Eggs, beaten
2	Cups	Biscuit mix
1	Cup	Sour cream
1/4	Tsp.	Salt
		Paprika

DIRECTIONS

Fry bacon until lightly browned.

Add onion and cook until transparent.

Add clams and clam liquid.

Season with salt and pepper.

Blend in flour and stir until sauce thickens.

Stir a little hot sauce into eggs, then add eggs to remaining sauce, stirring constantly.

Prepare biscuit mix.

Roll out biscuit mix and line a 9" pie pan. Flute edges.

Pour clam filling into shell.

Combine sour cream with 1/4 teaspoon salt and spread on top.

Sprinkle with paprika.

Bake in preheated 350 degree oven for 30 minutes.

Creamy Clam Pie

INGREDIENTS (serves 6)

1	Package	Pie crust mix
2	Tbls.	Bread crumbs
2	Cups	Clams, minced, with liquid
1/2	Cup	Light cream or milk
2	Tbls.	Butter
1/2	Cup	Onion, diced
1/4	Cup	Flour
1/2	Tsp.	Salt
1/4	Tsp.	Pepper
1/2	Tsp.	Celery salt
2	Cups	Potatoes, cooked, peeled and cut into 3/8" cubes

DIRECTIONS

Prepare pie crust mix, following label directions. Roll out half into a 12" round on a lightly floured surface. Fit into a 9" pie plate. Trim overhang to 1/2". Wet outside 1" of top with water.

Sprinkle bread crumbs over bottom.

Drain clams. Add enough water to make 1 cup of liquid in a 2 cup measure. Add cream.

Melt butter in saucepan and slowly saute onions until transparent.

Stir in flour. Gradually add clam liquid and cream, stirring constantly, until a thick creamy sauce is formed.

Add seasonings, clams and potatoes. Pour into pie shell.

Roll out remaining pastry into an 11" round. Cover pie. Trim overhang to 1/2" and turn edges under, flush with rim. Flute to make a stand-up edge. Brush with beaten egg or milk to make a shiny crust. Cut decorative slits in top to allow steam to escape.

Bake in a preheated 375 degree oven for 40 minutes, or until golden.

Let stand 15 minutes before serving.

Clam Hash

INGREDIENTS (serves 4)

4	Tbls.	Butter
4	Slices	Bacon, chopped
1	Cup	Onion, chopped
1	Cup	Clams, minced, drained of liquid
2	Cups	Potatoes, cooked peeled and diced
1/4	Cup	Parsley, chopped
1/4	Tsp.	Salt
1/8	Tsp.	Pepper
4	Tbls.	Grated Parmesan cheese

DIRECTIONS

Melt butter in skillet.

Add bacon and fry until crisp. Drain bacon on absorbent paper.

Saute onion until transparent.

Add potatoes, clams, parsley, salt and pepper. Press down with a spatula and cook over moderately high heat until bottom is brown.

Turn it with the spatula, mixing some of the crust throughout.

Press down again and cook until bottom is again brown.

Top with the cheese and bacon bits.

Cover tightly and cook for about 1 minute, until cheese melts.

Serve immediately, garnished with a parsley sprig.

Baked Clam Hash

INGREDIENTS (serves 6)

1/3	Cup	Bacon, chopped
1/2	Cup	Onion, chopped
2	Cups	Clams, minced and drained of liquid
4	Cups	Potatoes, cooked peeled and diced
1/4	Cup	Parsley
2		Eggs, beaten
2	Tsp.	Salt
1/8	Tsp.	Pepper
1/8	Tsp.	Paprika

DIRECTIONS

Fry bacon until crisp. Drain on absorbent paper.

Saute onions in bacon fat until transparent.

Add clams and cook until clams are heated through.

Add potatoes, parsley, eggs, salt and pepper.

Mix lightly and place in a well-greased baking pan, 11" x 7" x 1 1/2".

Sprinkle with paprika and bake in a preheated 350 degree oven for 30 to 35 minutes.

Garnish with bacon bits.

Clam Pilaf

INGREDIENTS (serves 4 to 6)

2	Dozen	Littleneck or cherrystone clams, cleaned
1	Cup	Dry white wine
1	Cup	Water
3	Tbls.	Butter
1	Medium	Onion, diced fine (about 1/2 cup)
1	Clove	Garlic, minced
1-1/2	Cups	Long-grain converted rice
1	Cup	Chicken broth
1/8	Tsp.	Salt
1/8	Tsp.	Black pepper, freshly ground
1/2	Tsp.	Ground oregano
1/4	Cup	Parsley flakes

DIRECTIONS

Place clams in a 4 quart saucepan. Add wine and water. Cover and bring to a boil over high heat. Steam clams for 5 to 8 minutes, shaking pan frequently, just until clams open. Strain liquid and reserve. Set clams aside.

Melt the butter in a heavy 2 quart saucepan over medium heat. Add onion and garlic. Saute for about 10 minutes, until onion is softened but not browned.

Add 2 cups of the clam liquid, the rice, broth, salt and pepper. Bring to a boil, stir once, reduce heat, cover and simmer slowly until all liquid is absorbed and rice is tender, about 15 minutes.

Meanwhile, shuck the clams, discarding any shells which did not open. Cut littlenecks in half and cherrystones into quarters.

When rice is done, remove from heat. Add clams and oregano. Stir gently and let stand, covered, for 10 minutes.

Taste and adjust seasonings. Stir in the parsley and transfer to a serving dish.

In a Supporting Role

Fish Boil

INGREDIENTS (serves 4)

2	Pounds	Fresh fish, cleaned and cut into 1" squares
4	Slices	Lemon
4	Slices	Orange
1	Pinch	Saffron
1/2	Tsp.	Salt
1/2	Tsp.	Black pepper, freshly ground
6		Cloves
1	Clove	Garlic, chopped
1	Pinch	Thyme
3	Tbls.	Parsley, chopped
2		Large onions, peeled and quartered
2		Large tomatoes, quartered
1/2	Cup	Olive oil
1	Fifth	Dry white wine
		Water
12		Clams, fresh, shucked
12		Shrimp, uncooked, peeled

DIRECTIONS

Put all ingredients through wine in a large kettle.

Add enough water to cover.

Cover kettle and bring to fast boil. Simmer for 15 minutes.

Add clams and shrimp. Cook for 5 minutes more.

Adjust seasonings.

Serve in large soup bowls with hot French bread.

Pork With Clams

INGREDIENTS (serves 6)

2	Pounds	Boneless pork loin, cut into 1" cubes
1 1/2	Cups	Dry white wine
1	Tbl.	Paprika
2		Bay leaves
3	Cloves	Garlic, split
1	Tsp.	Salt
1/4	Tsp.	Pepper
5	Tbls.	Lard
2	Cloves	Garlic, minced
1	Cup	Onions, thinly sliced
1	Cup	Green pepper, cut into julienne strips
2		Tomatoes, peeled, seeded and chopped
1	Tsp.	Salt
1/8	Tsp.	Cayenne pepper
1/8	Tsp.	Black pepper, freshly ground
36		Littleneck clams, well scrubbed

DIRECTIONS

In a large glass or ceramic bowl, combine pork, wine, paprika, bay leaves, split garlic, salt and pepper. Cover and place in refrigerator. Marinate for 8 hours, turning ingredients occasionally.

Discard bay leaves and garlic. Transfer pork cubes to paper towel and pat dry. Reserve marinade.

Melt 3 tablespoons lard in a large skillet. Cook pork at high heat until browned and cooked through. Transfer pork to heated dish and keep warm.

Add remaining marinade to skillet and stir in the brown bits clinging to the bottom of the pan. Reduce marinade by half and pour over pork.

In skillet, melt 2 tablespoons lard. Saute minced garlic, onions and peppers until soft.

Add tomatoes, salt and peppers. Cook for 3 minutes.

Add clams. Cover and cook for 3 to 5 minutes, or until clams open.

Add pork cubes and the marinade. Cook for 2 to 3 minutes until hot.

Place mixture on heated serving dish. Garnish with fresh coriander or parsley and lemon slices.

Cioppino

INGREDIENTS (serves 6 to 8)

1/4	Cup	Olive oil
4	Tbls.	Butter
3	Cloves	Garlic, finely chopped
1 1/4	Cups	Onion, chopped
3/4	Cup	Green pepper, chopped
1	Can	Tomatoes (28 onces)
1	Can	Tomato paste (6 ounces)
1		Bay leaf
1/3	Cup	Parsley, chopped
2	Tsp.	Oregano
1/2	Tsp.	Basil
2	Tsp.	Salt
1/4	Tsp.	Pepper
2	Cups	Dry wine
1 1/2	Pounds	Fish, cleaned, boned and cut into 2" pieces (sea bass, halibut, rockfish or any other fish that will form firm flakes when cooked)
1/2	Pound	Raw shrimp, cleaned and deveined
1/2	Pound	Scallops, fresh or frozen
1/2	Pound	Crabmeat, cooked
1	Dozen	Littleneck or cherrystone clams, well scrubbed, in shells

DIRECTIONS

Heat olive oil and butter in a skillet.

Saute garlic, onion and pepper until soft.

Place this mixture into a 6 quart kettle and add tomatoes, tomato paste, bay leaf, parsley, oregano, basil, salt and pepper.

Bring to a boil, lower heat and simmer for 2 hours, stirring occasionally. Discard bay leaf.

Stir wine into sauce. Add fish, shrimp and scallops. Simmer, covered, for 10 minutes.

Add crabmeat and lay clams on top of sauce. Cover and simmer for 5 minutes longer, or until clam shells have opened and fish flakes easily.

Serve immediately in wide soup bowls, with a little parsley sprinkled on top. Serve with a tossed salad and garlic bread.

HINT

Don't try to adhere to the specified seafoods too strictly. This dish is a specialty around Fisherman's Wharf in San Francisco where Italian fishermen created it from whatever they caught, added to a rich Italian tomato sauce. So, feel at liberty to:

Use a whole, large crab, cooked, cleaned and cracked, rather than the crabmeat.

Either add or substitute mussels or oysters for the clams.

Top off the pot with a couple of 1 1/2 pound lobsters, which have been boiled, split and with claws cracked.

If you don't have any fresh seafood, use frozen or canned.

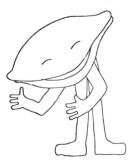

Paella

INGREDIENTS (serves 6)

1/3	Cup	Olive oil
2 1/2	Pounds	Frying chicken, cut in pieces
1/2	Pound	Chorizo (Spanish sausage), sweet Italian sausage or garlic-seasoned smoked sausage, cut into 1" pieces
1	Pound	Shrimp, cooked, peeled and deveined
1	Pound	Lobster tails, cut into 1" sections, in shell
3	Cloves	Garlic, slivered
2		Onions, about 2", cut in eighths
1		Green pepper, seeded and cut in 1" pieces
1	Cup	Clam juice
1	Cup	Dry white wine
1	Cup	Chicken stock
1	Cup	Pimiento, sliced
1	Tsp.	Saffron, crumbled
1	Tbl.	Paprika
1	Tsp.	Oregano
1	Tsp.	Salt
1/4	Tsp.	Pepper
1 1/2	Cups	Uncooked white rice
2		Tomatoes, 2", peeled and cut in eights
12		Hard shelled clams, small, well scrubbed
1/2	Cup	Peas, frozen (1/2 package)

DIRECTIONS

Heat oil in large heavy skillet.

Brown the chicken pieces in oil and remove.

Brown the sausage pieces in oil and remove.

Brown the shrimp pieces in oil and remove.

Brown the lobster pieces in oil and remove.

Add garlic, onion and pepper to skillet and saute lightly.

Add clam juice, wine, chicken stock, pimiento, saffron, paprika, oregano, salt, pepper and rice.

Bring mixture to a boil, stir once, then lay tomatoes, chicken, sausage and lobster on top.

Cover with foil and bake in a preheated 350 degree oven for 30 minutes.

Arrange clams and shrimp and scatter peas on top of mixture.

Cover and bake 15 minutes longer, or until liquid is absorbed and rice is tender.

HINT

This is the way I like paella, but it's actually a dish that has as many variations as it has cooks. The essential ingredients are rice, saffron, pimento and onions. After that, you're on your own to add whatever you like of what's available.

Paella may also be cooked completely on top of the stove. If you select this method, omit the final four directions in the recipe above and proceed as follows:

Bring mixture to a boil, stir once, then reduce heat so that the liquid barely simmers.

Lay tomatoes, chicken, sausage, lobster, clams and shrimp on top.

Scatter peas on top of this mixture.

Simmer slowly, tending pan frequently, and checking pan bottom to prevent scorching.

Cook until rice is tender and has absorbed all liquid, or about 40 minutes.

Bouillabaisse

INGREDIENTS (serves about 10)

1/2	Cup	Olive oil
1	Clove	Garlic, minced
1/2	Cup	Onion, chopped
1/2	Cup	Carrot, sliced thin
1/2	Cup	Celery, sliced thin
2	Cups	Tomatoes, peeled and cut up
1	Bottle	Clam juice (8 ounces)
1	Tsp.	Sage
1	Tsp.	Thyme
1/2	Tsp.	Saffron
2		Bay leaves
1	Tbl.	Salt
1	Tsp.	Paprika
1/8	Tsp.	Cayenne pepper
2 1/2	Cups	Water
1	Cup	Dry sherry
2	Pounds	Rock lobster tails, cut into 1" sections
1	Pound	Each perch, cod, rock, sole and red snapper; cleaned, deboned and cut into 2" pieces
1	Pound	Fresh shrimp, with shell removed and deveined
1	Cup	Crabmeat, cooked
2	Dozen	Small hard shell clams, well scrubbed

DIRECTIONS

Heat oil in a large dutch oven. Add garlic, onion, carrot, celery, tomatoes, clam juice, sage, thyme, saffron, bay leaves, salt, paprika pepper and water.

Bring to a boil, lower heat and simmer for 15 minutes.

Stir in the sherry.

Layer in the lobster, each type of fish and the shrimp. Cover and simmer for 10 minutes longer.

Add crabmeat and clams. Cover and simmer for 5 minutes longer, or until the clams open and fish flakes easily.

Serve immediately, in wide soup bowls, with a little parsley sprinkled on top. Serve with French bread and encourage dunking.

Riesling Seafood Shells

INGREDIENTS (serves 6 to 8)

1	Package	Frozen puff pastry shells
2	Tbls.	Butter
1	Cup	Mushrooms, diced
1	Cup	Lobster meat, diced
1	Cup	Shrimp, boiled, skinned, deveined and diced
1	Tbl.	Clams, drained and diced
1	Tbl.	Flour
1/2	Tsp.	Salt
1/8	Tsp.	Pepper, freshly ground
1/8	Tsp.	Garlic powder
1/8	Tsp.	Ground nutmeg
1 1/2	Cups	Riesling, chablis or other white dinner wine
1	Cup	Light cream
1/2	Cup	Parsley, chopped

DIRECTIONS

Bake puff pastry shells according to package directions. Remove centers and save for topping.

Dust the mushrooms and seafood with flour, salt, pepper, garlic and nutmeg.

Melt butter in saucepan. Lightly saute mushrooms and seafood.

Add wine and simmer for 10 minutes.

Add cream and heat to just below simmer.

Adjust seasonings.

Pour into pastry shells. Sprinkle with parsley.

Top with reserved pastry covers and serve.

Baked Flounder With Clam Sauce

INGREDIENTS (serves 4)

1 1/2	Pounds	Fillet of flounder or sole
1		Onion, about 1" in diameter, finely diced
1	Cup	Clams, minced (reserve liquid)
2/3	Cup	Dry white wine
2	Tbls.	Butter
1 1/2	Tbls.	Flour
1/2	Cup	Heavy cream
		Salt
		White pepper

DIRECTIONS

Arrange fillets in a shallow baking dish. Sprinkle with onion.

To clam liquid, add enough wine to make 1 cup. Pour over fillets.

Bake in a preheated 325 degree oven until just done, about 15 minutes.

Carefully transfer fillets to a heatproof serving dish and keep warm.

Melt butter in a saucepan and stir in flour.

Gradually stir in 1 cup of hot cooking liquid, the heavy cream and the clams.

Season to taste with salt and white pepper.

Heat until hot but not boiling and pour over cooked fillets.

Broil, about 4" from heat, for about 4 minutes, until the sauce bubbles and begins to glaze.

Serve immediately.

Fillet of Sole With Parmesan Cheese

INGREDIENTS (serves 4)

4		Fillets of sole
2	Tsp.	Salt
1/2	Tsp.	Pepper, freshly ground
6	Tbls.	Butter
1/2	Cup	Parmesan cheese
1/4	Cup	Clam juice

DIRECTIONS

Wash and dry the fillets.

Season with salt and pepper.

Melt 4 tablespoons butter in a skillet and saute fish until browned on both sides.

Add the clam juice, sprinkle with the cheese and dot with remaining butter.

Cover and cook over low heat for 5 minutes.

Serve hot with lemon wedges.

Shrimp, Lake Como Style

INGREDIENTS (serves 4 to 6)

3	Tbls.	Olive oil
3	Tbls.	Butter
1/4	Cup	Onion, minced
2	Tbls.	Carrot, grated
1	Clove	Garlic, minced
1		Bay leaf
1 1/2	Pounds	Shrimp, raw, shelled and deveined
1	Tsp.	Salt
1/4	Tsp.	Black pepper, freshly ground
1/3	Cup	Cognac, warmed
1	Cup	Tomatoes, peeled and chopped
1/8	Tsp.	Oregano
1/8	Tsp.	Basil
3/4	Cup	Clam juice
1	Tbl.	Lemon juice
1	Tsp.	Flour
3/4	Cup	Heavy cream

DIRECTIONS

Heat the oil and 2 tablespoons butter in a skillet.

Add the onion, carrot, garlic and bay leaf. Saute for 10 minutes.

Add shrimp, salt and pepper. Saute for 3 minutes.

Pour cognac over the shrimp and set it aflame.

When flames die, add tomatoes, oregano, basil, clam and lemon juices. Cook over low heat for 8 minutes.

Remove shrimp to a warm serving dish. Remove and discard bay leaf.

Cook the sauce over high heat for 2 minutes.

Cream the flour with the remaining butter and add to the sauce with the cream.

Cook over low heat for 3 minutes, stirring steadily.

Pour the sauce over the shrimp and serve immediately.

Chicken With Clams

INGREDIENTS (serves 4)

1	Cup	Clams, minced, with liquid
4		Chicken breasts, boned and skinned
1	Cup	Clam broth
1 1/2	Tbls.	Butter, softened
1 1/2	Tbls.	Flour
1/4	Tsp.	Salt
1/8	Tsp.	Pepper
1/8	Tsp	Nutmeg
		Parsley for garnish

DIRECTIONS

Drain clams and reserve liquid.

Lay chicken breasts side by side in a heavy skillet. Add liquid from clams and the clam broth. Cover and simmer for 25 minutes, until chicken is very tender.

Remove chicken to a serving dish and keep it warm.

Mix butter and flour to a paste. Add it bit by bit to the clam broth in the skillet. Cook, stirring until sauce thickens.

Add minced clams, salt, pepper and nutmeg. Simmer for 1 minute.

Adjust seasonings and pour over chicken. Garnish with a sprig of parsley.

Bonus Chapter

Baked Stuffed Clams

INGREDIENTS (makes 8 appetizers)

1	Can	Minced clams (6-1/2 ounces), drained
1-1/2	Cups	Soft bread crumbs (3 slices)
1/4	Cup	Grated cheese (1 ounce)
1	Tbl.	Parsley flakes
1/4	Tsp.	Garlic salt
2	Tbls.	Olive oil or salad oil
1	Tsp.	Lemon juice

DIRECTIONS

Combine all ingredients in a small bowl and toss lightly to mix.

Spoon into 8 scrubbed clam shells or small foil muffin pan cups.
Place filled shells onto a baking sheet for easy handling. Chill if made
ahead.

Bake, just before serving, in a preheated 375° oven, for 15 minutes,
or until hot and golden.

Baked Stuffed Cherrystone Clams

INGREDIENTS (makes 20 to 24 appetizers)

36		Cherrystone clams
1	Tsp.	Nutmeg
1	Tsp.	Mace
2-1/2	Cups	Dry bread crumbs
8	Tbls.	Butter (1 stick)

DIRECTIONS

Shuck the clams. Reserve any captured clam juice for another use. Either leave the clams whole or mince them. Wash and dry about 48 of the largest half-shells.

Sprinkle the clams with the nutmeg and mace. Toss to blend.

Butter the bottom and sides of a 2 quart baking dish. Sprinkle a layer of bread crumbs into the bottom, and dot generously with the butter. Add a layer of clams, either whole or minced. Next, another layer of bread crumbs and dots of butter. Proceed until ingredients have been used, ending with a layer of bread crumbs on top.

Bake, in a preheated 375° oven, for about 15 minutes. Fill the reserved clam shells with this mixture, either leaving them open or covering each with another clam shell.

Arrange the stuffed clams on a baking sheet and return them to the oven for 5 minutes. Transfer them to a serving dish and serve them piping hot.

Broiled Stuffed Clams

INGREDIENTS (serves 4)

12	Large	Hard shelled clams, 3" to 4" across
1/2	Cup	Dry white wine
1	Stick	Butter, softened
1	Large	Shallot, minced
1	Clove	Garlic, minced
1	Tbl.	Parsley flakes
1	Tsp.	Cognac
1	Tsp.	Ricard (or other anise-flavored liqueur)
1/8	Tsp.	Salt
1/8	Tsp.	Black pepper, freshly ground
12	Tbls.	Dry bread crumbs
2	Tbls.	Ricard

DIRECTIONS

Bring the wine to a boil in a large stainless steel saucepan. Add the clams, and steam them, covered, for 10 minutes, until the shells have opened. Discard any unopened shells. Shuck the clams, reserving the bottom half of each shell. Cut each clam into quarters and place 4 quarters into each bottom shell.

In a bowl, cream together the butter, shallot, garlic, parsley, Cognac, Ricard, salt and pepper. Divide the butter mixture among the clams, covering them completely.

Sprinkle each with a tablespoon of bread crumbs, and arrange them on a large baking sheet which has been covered with a layer of coarse salt to keep the clams from tipping.

Broil them, about 4" from heat source, for 3 to 5 minutes, or until crumbs are golden and sauce is bubbly.

Divide the clams among 4 serving dishes. Heat the Ricard until hot in a small saucepan. Ignite it, and pour over the clams. Serve immediately.

Fried Stuffed Clams

INGREDIENTS (makes 18 appetizers)

24		Cherrystone clams, cleaned
1/2	Tsp.	Salt
2	Tbls.	Olive oil
1	Medium	Onion, diced fine (about 1/2 cup)
4	Cloves	Garlic, minced
1/4	Cup	Parsley flakes
2	Tsps.	Dried oregano
1/4	Tsp.	Salt
1/8	tsp.	Black pepper, freshly ground
1	Dash	Cayenne pepper
3	Tbls.	Butter
1/4	Cup	Flour
1/2	Cup	Milk
2		Eggs
1	Cup	Dry bread crumbs
2	Tbls.	Grated Parmesan cheese
		Oil (for deep frying)

DIRECTIONS

Place the clams into a large pot, together with the salt and 1/2 cup of water. Steam the clams, over high heat, shaking the pot frequently, for 5 to 8 minutes, just until clams open.

Drain liquid and reserve. Remove clam meat and mince. Discard any shells which have not opened. Rinse and dry 18 half-shells.

Heat the olive oil in a small skillet over medium-high heat. Add onion and saute until transparent, about 5 minutes. Mix in the garlic, parsley flakes, oregano, salt, black and cayenne peppers, and cook for 2 minutes.

Remove from heat and stir in the minced clams. Divide the mixture evenly among the reserved clam shells.

Melt butter in a small saucepan over medium heat. Stir in the flour until well blended. Gradually add 1/2 cup of reserved clam liquid and the milk, stirring constantly, until sauce is very thick and smooth. Remove from heat and let cool, stirring occasionally.

Spoon sauce over clam mixture, spreading to edges. Refrigerate the stuffed clams for 1 hour or more.

Beat the eggs in a small bowl. Combine bread crumbs and Parmesan in another. Add oil to a depth of 1" in a skillet and heat to 375°.

continued

Dip stuffed clams, filled side down, into eggs, then into bread crumb mixture. Carefully add clams, in batches, filled side down, to skillet (if oil is too hot clam shells may shatter). Fry until well browned. Let drain on paper towels. Transfer to platter and serve.

NOTE: Clams may be prepared ahead and kept warm in a 200° oven for 30 minutes.

Steamed Stuffed Clams

INGREDIENTS (serves 6)

18		Cherrystone clams, cleaned
1/2	Tsp.	Salt
1/2	Pound	Pork, finely ground
1/4	Cup	Fresh mushrooms, diced
1	Tbl.	Soy sauce
1	Tbl.	Chablis
1	Tbl.	Cornstarch
1	Tbl.	Scallion, minced
1	Tbl.	Ginger root, peeled and minced
1/2	Tsp.	Sesame oil
1/2	Tsp.	Salt

DIRECTIONS

Place the clams into a large pot together with the salt and 1/2 cup of water. Place over high heat and steam the clams for about 5 minutes, shaking the pot frequently, just until the clams open.

Drain the clams. Remove clams from the shells, discarding any shells that have not opened. Mince the clams. Rinse and dry 18 half-shells.

In a mixing bowl, combine clams and all the remaining ingredients. Mix well, and toss the mixture lightly against the inside of the bowl to combine and compact it.

With a spoon dipped in cold water, stuff the reserved shells with this mixture, mounding it and smoothing it.

Arrange the clams on a tray in a steamer and steam for 20 minutes.

Creamy Clams on the Half Shell

INGREDIENTS (serves 4)

12	Large	Hard shell clams, 3" to 4" across, cleaned
2	Tbls.	Butter
3	Tbls.	Flour
3/4	Cup	Milk
1		Egg yolk
1	Tbl.	Parsley flakes
1	Tbl.	Onion, diced fine
1/8	Tsp.	Black pepper, freshly ground
2	Tbls.	Grated Parmesan cheese
1	Cup	Dried bread crumbs
2	Tbls.	Butter, melted

DIRECTIONS

Shuck the clams. Save 12 half-shells. Dry the half-shells and coat the insides with butter. Coarsely chop the clams. Drain clams and reserve the juice for another use.

Melt the butter in a small saucepan. Add the flour and stir until smooth. Gradually add the milk, stirring constantly, until thickened.

Beat the egg yolk. Add some of the hot sauce to the yolk. Pour the yolk mixture back into the sauce and cook for 1 minute, stirring constantly.

Stir in the parsley, onion, pepper and drained clams.

Pile this misture into the buttered clam shells and sprinkle them with cheese. Blend bread crumbs with butter and sprinkle over the cheese.

Arrange clams on a baking sheet and broil, 4" from heat source, for 10 minutes. Serve hot.

Jellied Clam and Vegetable Soup

INGREDIENTS (serves 4)

1	Envelope	Unflavored Gelatin (1 tablespoon)
1/2	Cup	Cold water
1	Cup	Clam juice (one 8 ounce bottle)
1/4	Tsp.	Worcestershire sauce
1/2	Tsp.	Salt
1/8	Tsp.	Black pepper, freshly ground
1	Dash	Cayenne pepper
1/2	Cup	Tomato (firm), chopped fine
1/2	Cup	Green pepper, chopped fine
1/2	Cup	Carrot, grated
1/4	Cup	Cucumber, grated
2	Tbls.	Fresh parsley, minced
2	Tbls.	Green onion, chopped fine
4	Wedges	Lemon

DIRECTIONS

Add gelatin to cold water and let stand for 5 minutes. In a small saucepan, heat the clam juice, and then remove from heat. Add soaked gelatin and stir until dissolved.

Stir in the Worcestershire sauce, salt, black and cayenne peppers.

Chill by setting in ice water until mixtue begins to set.

Fold in the tomato, green pepper, carrot, cucumber, parsley and onion.

Chill until set.

At serving time, break up the mixture slightly with a fork. Spoon into chilled soup cups. Garnish with lemon wedges.

Red Chowder with Thyme

INGREDIENTS (serves 6 to 8)

4	Dozen	Cherrystone clams, cleaned
1	Can	Italian plum tomatoes (28 ounces), chopped coarse, including juice
1-1/2	Cups	Clam juice (bottled)
1/4	Cup	Tomato paste
2	Tsps.	Dried thyme
1/2	Tsp.	Dried marjoram
1		Bay leaf
1/8	Tsp.	Cayenne pepper
1/4	Tsp.	Salt
1/8	Tsp.	Black pepper, freshly ground
4	Tbls.	Butter
3	Large	Boiling potatoes, peeled and diced into 1/2" cubes
1	Large	Onion, diced (about 1 cup)
2	Large	Celery stalks, diced
1/4	Cup	Parsley flakes

DIRECTIONS

In a kettle, steam the clams in 1 cup water over moderately high heat for about 5 minutes, until they open. Transfer the clams to a bowl, discarding any clams which do not open. Coarsely chop the clams.

Strain the liquid through a fine sieve, which has been lined with a double layer of rinsed and squeezed cheesecloth, into a large stainless steel saucepan. Add the tomatoes, clam juice, tomato paste, thyme, marjoram, bay leaf, cayenne, salt and pepper.

Heat the butter in a large skillet, and then add the potatoes, onion and celery, Saute for about 10 minutes, stirring occasionally, until onion and celery are soft. Add this mixture to the saucepan containing the tomatoes.

Bring the mixture to a boil and simmer, covered, for about 20 minutes, until potatoes are soft. Add the clams, bring the chowder to a simmer, and then add the parsley. Remove the bay leaf.

The chowder is ready to eat now, or may be chilled for reheating at a later time.

Sausage and Clam Soup

INGREDIENTS (serves 6 to 8)

1/4	Cup	Olive oil
1	Pound	Hot Italian sausage, casings removed
1	Pound	Fresh mushrooms, coarsely chopped
2	Medium	Onions, sliced (about 1 cup)
1	Can	Whole peeled Italian tomatoes (28 ounces), undrained
1	Cup	Dry white wine
1	Cup	Clam juice (fresh or bottled)
2	Tsps.	Dried basil
1	Tbl.	Garlic, minced
1	Large	Bunch of parsley, stems removed, chopped
6	Dozen	Littleneck clams, scrubbed

DIRECTIONS

Heat olive oil in a large Dutch oven, over medium heat. Add sausage, mushrooms and onions. Cook, stirring frequently, while breaking up the sausages with a fork, until sausage loses its pink color, about 10 minutes.

Stir in the tomatoes. Bring mixture to a boil, crushing tomatoes into small pieces. Reduce heat to low and simmer for 5 minutes.

Pour in wine and clam juice. Return mixture to a boil. Reduce heat to low, cover and simmer for 20 minutes, stirring occasionally.

Add basil and garlic, and cook for 5 minutes more.*

Transfer stock to a pot large enough to accomodate both stock and clams. (If a large pot is not available, use two pots and divide ingredients evenly). Bring to a boil over high heat. Add half the parsley to pot and reserve remaining half.

Add clams. Reduce heat to medium high, cover and simmer until clams open, about 5 to 10 minutes. Ladle soup into bowls and garnish with remaining parsley. Discard any clams which do not open. Serve immediately.

*Stock can be prepared 1 day ahead to this point, covered and refrigerated until ready to serve.

Clam Gumbo

INGREDIENTS (serves 4 to 6)

1/4	Pound	Salt pork or bacon, diced
2	Tbls.	Butter
1	Small	Onion, diced
1	Clove	Garlic, minced
2	Cups	Okra, sliced (may be fresh, frozen and thawed, or canned)
1	Can	Tomatoes (16 ounces), with juice
3	Cups	Water
1/4		Lemon, thinly sliced, seeds removed
1		Bay leaf
1/2	Tsp.	Salt
1/4	Tsp.	Paprika
1/8	Tsp.	Tabasco sauce
1	Tsp.	Worcestershire sauce
2	Tbls.	Butter
2	Tbls.	Flour
4	Cans	Minced clams (6-1/2 ounces each), drained

DIRECTIONS

In a heavy kettle, cook the salt pork over medium heat until fat has been rendered. Add the butter, onion and garlic. Cook, stirring frequently, until onion is transparent.

Add the okra, tomatoes, water, lemon, bay leaf, salt, paprika, Tabasco and Worcestershire sauces. Bring to a boil, lower the heat, and simmer for 1 hour.

Blend the remaining butter with the flour and stir this mixture, bit by bit, into the simmering vegetables, until thickened and smooth.

Stir in the minced clams and heat to boiling. Serve with steamed rice.

Clam Fritters

INGREDIENTS (makes about 30 fritters)

15		Cherrystone clams, cleaned, shucked, and coarsely chopped
2/3	Cup	All purpose flour
1/3	Cup	Milk
1	Small	Egg, beaten lightly
1	Small	Onion, minced (about 1/4 cup)
1-1/8	Tsp.	Baking powder
1/4	Tsp.	Salt
1/4	Tsp.	Tabasco sauce
1	Clove	Garlic, minced
2	Tsps.	Parsley flakes
1/8	Tsp.	Dried thyme
1/8	Tsp.	Dried basil
		Vegetable oil (for frying)

DIRECTIONS

Combine all ingredients except vegetable oil in a large mixing bowl, and mix well. Chill the batter, covered, for 2 hours.

Heat the vegetable oil, 3" deep, in a deep fat fryer to a temperature of 375°. Fry tablespoons of the batter, in batches, turning them for 3 or 4 minutes as they brown. As they are fried, transfer them with a skimmer to paper towels to drain.

Keep the fritters warm in a preheated 200° oven until ready to serve.

Clams Oreganata

INGREDIENTS (serves 4)

3	Tbls.	Olive oil
1	Cup	Onion, chopped
2	Tbls.	Dried oregano leaves
1	Cup	Dry white wine
1/8	Tsp.	Salt
1/8	Tsp.	Black pepper, freshly ground
2	Pounds	Littleneck clams, scrubbed
2	Tbls.	Parsley flakes
8		Lemon wedges

DIRECTIONS

In a 6-quart saucepan, heat the oil until hot but not smoking. Add the onion and saute, stirring frequently, until onion is transparent but not brown, about 5 minutes.

Add the oregano and toss with the onion. Stir in the wine and simmer until reduced by half. Season with the salt and pepper.

Carefully place the clams in the pan and cover tightly. Steam, shaking the pan occasionally, just until the clams open, about 6 to 8 minutes. Discard any clams that do not open.

Serve in large soup plates, garnished with the parsley flakes and lemon wedges.

Clams in Black Bean Sauce

INGREDIENTS (serves 6)

1	Tbl.	Peanut oil
2	Tsps.	Fresh ginger root, peeled and diced
1	Clove	Garlic, diced
1		Dried hot pepper, chopped
1/2	Cup	Preserved black beans, well rinsed*
1/4	Cup	Water
1	Tsp.	Dry sherry
1	Tsp.	Soy sauce
1/2	Tsp.	Sesame oil*
3	Dozen	Littleneck clams, cleaned
3	Tbls.	Green onion, chopped fine

DIRECTIONS

Heat oil in a small frying pan over medium-high heat. Add ginger, garlic and red pepper. Saute until lightly browned. With a slotted spoon, remove ginger, garlic and red pepper pieces and discard.

Stir in the black beans and water. Bring to a boil. Season with sherry, soy sauce and sesame oil. Remove from heat and keep warm. (Sauce may be prepared ahead and reheated).

Place clams in a large pot. Add 1 cup of water, cover and place over high heat. Bring to a boil and steam for 5 to 8 minutes, shaking pot frequently, just until clams open.

Drain clams thoroughly, Discard top shell and any clams which do not open. Arrange 6 clams on each serving dish.

Stir sauce well and spoon over the clams. Garnish with the green onion.

*Available at Oriental markets.